What Will Have Happened

ROBERT CHAMPIGNY

What Will Have Happened

a philosophical
and technical essay
on mystery stories

Indiana University Press   Bloomington   London

Published in Canada by Fitzhenry & Whiteside Limited, Don Mills, Ontario

Manufactured in the United States of America

Library of Congress Cataloging in Publication Data
Champigny, Robert, 1922–
    What will have happened.
    Includes bibliographical references.
    1. Detective and mystery stories—Technique.
I. Title.
PN3377.5.D4C5   808.3'872   77–74446
ISBN 0–253–36515–5   1   2   3   4   5   81   80   79   78   77

To David Hayman

Contents

viii / *Contents*

What Will Have Happened

Prologue

NARRATIVE SENTENCES may be interpreted as indicating historical or fictional events. In the former case, what is narrated is spatiotemporally related to the interpreter's own incarnation; in the latter case, it is not. In the former case, the sentences are taken to be more or less true or false statements, liable to verification. In the latter case, the sentences are accepted as neither true nor false axioms; what can be checked is the coherence. The "historicizing" mode of meaning and interpretation is cognitive and practical; the "fictionalizing" mode is ludic (playful) and esthetic.

The adoption of one of the two kinds of interpretation depends on the peculiarities of the text and on the interpreter's background. It may even depend on his mood. I may view as history a text which the author intended to be a biography of a historical ("real") individual. But I may also discard the true-or-false perspective and choose to appreciate the text as if its material had been invented. My perspective may even shift from one kind of interpretation to the other as my reading proceeds. The texts under discussion in this essay will be regarded as projecting fictional events.

When they are read for the first time, mystery stories orient the attention toward some events whose determination is held in suspense until the last pages. Certain assumptions or hypotheses concerning these events are then rejected as "false." (In order to avoid confusion with what is cognitively [historically] true or false, the words "true" and "false" had better be kept within antiseptic quotation marks when they apply to fiction. One may also speak of valid or invalid axioms.)

The intrinsic interest of a piece of narrative fiction is ludic and esthetic. When it is read for the first time, the interest is broadly ludic. One wonders what the text is up to, how it is going to shape up. The text functions as both teammate and opponent of the reader. If it is reread, and if the reader has retained a notion of the whole, the interest becomes more narrowly "esthetic." Each part can be appreciated in relation to what follows it as well as to what precedes it. Rereading allows a greater intimacy with the text, and I would define the ideal of esthetic enjoyment as a coincidence between the reader and the text as a whole at every moment. However, esthetic enjoyment should not be confused with mystical trance. The fusion between reader and text into a depersonified act of meaning subdues but does not eliminate cognitive and practical consciousness, the position of oneself as a "real person" reading a text at a certain time in a geographical place.

Mystery stories are designed to sharpen the ludic

interest. Either from the start or gradually, they delimit the content of the ending while keeping its particulars in the dark. As he reads the text for the first time, the reader is incited to wonder about not just what will happen but also what will have happened.

The question may arise whether this peculiar form may not be detrimental to esthetic appreciation if the text is reread. On the basis of my tastes, I should say that most of the mystery stories I read are not worth rereading. But I would say the same about any kind of text, and I see nothing esthetically wrong with the mystery genre itself. To my mind, a heightened ludic interest is not necessarily detrimental to a narrowly esthetic enjoyment, since I consider esthetic value to be a refinement and confirmation of ludic value. In one way, reading and rereading offer markedly different perspectives in the case of mystery stories, if one remembers the denouement. But in another way, mystery stories make the two perspectives more similar, because on first reading they convey a more precise idea of the narrative goal than straight stories usually do.

I shall have to pay more attention to a first-reading perspective than I did in *Ontology of the Narrative,* an essay which dealt with the narrative mode in general. But this simply means an emphasis on the relations between the denouement and the rest of the text. I shall remain chiefly concerned with esthetic appreciation. A critical essay stems from a rereading experience. To analyze a text as if one were in the process of reading it for the first time can only be a cumbersome and misleading pretence. This is particularly noticeable in *S/Z,* by Roland

Barthes. The way in which he comments on Balzac's *Sarrasine,* sentence after sentence, is obviously informed by an acquaintance with the whole.

One may enjoy watching a game and not be partial to televised replays. Similarly, some readers may prefer to read texts, mystery stories in particular, only once and dispense with commentaries. I have no objection to this kind of preference. But my outlook is based on a rereading experience and on the principle that an esthetic, not just ludic enjoyment can be derived from a mystery story. Accordingly, some of my analyses will break a rule by which most reviewers abide: I shall disclose the denouement.

My essay will deal mostly with stylistic matters. But it will encroach on ontology, ethics, and epistemology, insofar as esthetics is related to these other philosophical branches. There follow a few preliminary indications concerning my general approach to these relationships.

The modes of meaning that I distinguish are modes of interpretation and comprehension. In phenomenological terms, they might be called modes of intentionality. But according to classical phenomenology, what is basically intended is always "the world": being-in-the-world is the root category. Some philosophers, whether they adopt the phenomenological label or not, conceive ontology to be an attempt to sketch the structure of "the world." This move tends to equate ontology with epistemology, what-is with what-is-to-be-known. This produces an uncomfortable status for ludic-esthetic modes of meaning, or intentionality. A fictional entity is not a "real" entity in an epistemological sense. Yet it is something. It must have some ontological status even though it has no epistemological standing.

I myself would grant a certain kind of priority to the "world," understood as the historical field of our practical incarnation, hence to epistemology and ethics over esthetics. Even if a ludic perspective is adopted, it remains framed by a cognitive and practical perspective. Otherwise, we could not distinguish between the fictional field of a performed drama and the field of its performance, between a character in the play and the actor in our practical field.

But inside the frame of ludic experience, what is basically intended is a fictional world, not the historical field. What is intended in general may be called "world" but only if this word is interpreted as a value term, as indicating something possessing "cosmicity" *(mundus, cosmos)*. If the meaning of "comprehension" is broadened and deepened enough to describe the basic need, then comprehension and cosmicity can be made to correspond.

In different yet connected ways, cognitive and ethical endeavors attempt to comprehend, to make sense of the historical and practical field, to make it cosmic. If they succeeded, ludic-esthetic activities would be deprived of a special *raison d'être.* These activities may be regarded as compensations or escapes, or even masks of cognitive and ethical failures. But at the same time they project the inaccessible ideals of cognitive and ethical aspirations. In this respect, esthetics may be granted a kind of priority over epistemology and ethics.

A narrative interpreted as fiction determines what it narrates axiomatically, thus representing the ideal of knowledge, of a cognition radically plagued with incompleteness and uncertainty. An esthetic intimacy with a narrative as a whole allows us partly to depersonify ourselves and enjoy the divine status of signifying act. As far as ethical sense is concerned, if every experience, animal and human, were lived under pure conditions of play, the moral ideal would be achieved. No doubt a piece of fiction may allude to the aspects of practical existence that lack moral sense (i.e., to evil), but fictional characters suffer fictionally. Thus any narrative, if it is interpreted as fiction, projects the moral ideal, whatever the content may be.

An ontological essay that ostensibly proposes to constitute being, or existence, as one totality ("the world") can only result in sketching the structure of a fictional cosmos. I prefer to play the ontological game differently: distinguish between modes of being, correlate them with modes of meaning. The systematic aspect would consist in founding, not totalizing. Philosophical reason should ration itself according to its own mode of meaning and ration other kinds of reason, other logics, other semantic functions. By itself, this plurality testifies to the impossibility of turning existence, or being, into one cosmic totality. It shows how philosophical reason is to limit sense with nonsense and antisense (being as antivalue). It would be inappropriate for an essay on mystery stories to develop a full-scale ontology. I shall confine founding operations to an appendix. Readers who are not partial to ontological games are advised to skip it.

The propositions of an essay are to be taken as neither true nor false, in a way that differs from narrative fiction since conceptualizing differs from narrating. Philosophy is not science. An essay should offer patterns of conceptual understanding, not cognitive models. Some essays claim that they are after "the truth"; they may even claim that they have found it. But the same kind of pretence, or pretension, has also been used in novels.

I view the philosophical mode of meaning as ludic. But I would not add that the ludic perspective should become narrowly esthetic if an essay is reread. An esthetic appreciation aims at an identification between text and interpreter within the frame of the experience. It appears to me that in order to maintain a philosophical attitude one must keep considering an essay as both teammate and adversary, even if one happens to feel a deep empathy with it.

An essay is "historical" to the extent that it is the result of human activities at a certain time in certain geographical places. But it is not a history; it is not an *Entwicklungsroman.* I shall not try to impose a narrative logic on my material; I shall not sketch the evolution of a character called *"the* mystery story." The material will be delimited conceptually, and I shall pick examples from various texts without regard for their dates of publication. Nor shall I attempt to link mystery stories to social, political, cultural, or ideological backgrounds, since such embroidery amounts to providing a character or a bunch of characters with an appropriately tailored setting. Apart from some brief allusions, I shall engage in this kind of sport only in an epilogue.

The examples will be drawn from texts written in English or French, as I do not feel qualified to make stylistic comments on texts written in other languages. Quotations from French texts will be translated; the French titles will be retained. The selection of texts to be mentioned and commented upon is less important in an essay than in a history. This does not mean, however, that my selection of examples is beyond the pale of criticism. Here and there the reader may decide that a text, which I did not read or failed to think of, would have illustrated a point better than the text I chose.

Part I / Mystery

Hermeneutic tales

I SHALL BE CONCERNED with texts that are coherently narrative. The narrated process will be considered as fictional. Mystery dramas and films will be left aside since their media are not purely linguistic.

A narrative is to be called a mystery story to the extent that the goal and result of the narrated process is the determination of some events anterior to the ending of the process. The mystery in a mystery story is a narrative secret, not a conceptual mystery; it is physical, not transcendental. A mystery story is a hermeneutic tale; I shall use these two labels interchangeably. A narrative that attracts the reader's attention to some undetermined events but avoids determining them at the end is not a mystery story in my sense, since it is not a hermeneutic tale. Unlike texts commonly called "adventure stories" or "suspense stories," mystery stories sharpen the interest not just for what will happen but for what will have happened. To some extent, in any narrative the description of an event further determines events already described. Mystery stories, however, radicalize the tension, or complementarity, between progressive and regressive determinations. This is what the future perfect in the phrase "what will have happened" is designed to suggest. Hermeneutic stories may also be said to radicalize the effect of the flashback device. The narrated process is oriented toward a retroactive denouement that should transfigure the whole sequence. Many mystery stories also sprinkle the development with hypotheses, that is to say, with tentative flashbacks, which will eventually be confirmed or rejected.

A story may unfold like a straight narrative and yet end with a deeply retroactive denouement. *The Spy Who Came In from the Cold,* by John Le Carré, does not make it clear to the reader that some decisive narrative axioms are being kept in suspense. Stories that do make this clear may, to varying degrees, conceal not only the solution but also what precisely constitutes the mystery. In any case it should be noted that, while certain indications are usually quite reliable, there can be no certainty that one is reading a hermeneutic tale before reaching the end.

Many mystery stories depict the successful efforts of a detective to identify a criminal, most often a murderer. But neither criminal nor detective is a necessary item. In *The Gold Bug,* by Edgar Allan Poe, the detective's goal is to determine the location of a buried treasure. In *The Blast of the Book,* by G. K. Chesterton, baffling disappearances turn out to be a hoax. In *And Then There Were None* (British title: *Ten Little Indians*), by Agatha Christie, the solution is generously given by the murderer. From the reader's standpoint, a hermeneutic tale has to be an investigation story, but the narrated process does not need a fictional investigator in order to function as an investigative sequence. Most of my examples will be drawn from texts in which a detective investigates a murder. But the delimitation of my topic does not necessitate this kind of content. It has to do with form, with a certain way of composing a narration. One of my purposes is to show that, far from being a marginal or outlandish species, mystery stories as defined above provide revealing tests of narrative logic and art.

Individuation

UNLIKE AN ESSAY or a poem, a fictionalizing narrative composes a spatiotemporal world. It builds processes out of events. The fictional world is the total process. Events may be regarded as simple individuals and processes as complex individuals. Narrating, spatiotemporalizing, and individuating will be used as equivalent terms.

Individuals (a blue dress, a tree) differ from universals (blue, treeness). Individuals are assumed to be spatially and temporally continuous. By themselves, universals are not spatiotemporal entities. Conceptual logic, which combines universals, differs from narrative logic, which combines individuals. But narration and conceptualization have to rely on each other, thus showing their ontological infirmities. There are various kinds of communications between individuals and universals, which may degenerate into idolatrous confusions.

Universals are spatiotemporalized as properties of individuals. And individuals step into the domain of universals under the guise of members of classes. The class of trees is infected by the spatiotemporal nature of its members: treeness includes patterns of irreversible change (growing, decaying) and periodicity (blooming, bearing fruit). Classes of individuals are patterns of individuation. The class of trees determines how individual tree processes should be composed. Causal laws may be regarded as rules for linking simple individuals: whenever an event belonging to class A occurs, it is followed by an event belonging to class B.

The proposition that a narrative "builds processes out of events" is somewhat misleading, since it suggests that the description of world points does not depend on the choice of world lines. In fact, descriptions of events normally present them as accidents of objects and parts of states of affairs, according to restrictions imposed by the syntax and vocabulary of a natural language. These linguistic models are more stringent than the limit imposed by physical science on the tracing of world lines (namely, the speed of light). Besides, in order to be a situated event and not just a bare phenomenon, what is described as something perceived or felt must be related to a complex individual who feels and perceives. Nonetheless, the proposition that a narrative builds processes out of events points to an important aspect: the description of an event may be narratively polysemic; it may allow different tracings of world lines, attributions of the event to different complex individuals within the constituted context. Mystery stories often exploit this kind of polysemy.

Some individuals are personified. What counts as a person is pretty hazy. Desire and self-recognition appear to be essential factors. The ability to address and be addressed through some semiotic medium would be an added condition. We are wont to personify some animals, especially those belonging to our own species. But even in our culture, personification occasionally oversteps these limits. We may have the impression that there is a desire at work in certain inanimate objects, that there is a spirit "in" a tree. We may believe in ghosts, we may personify what is divine. Most often, personification goes with individuation: one human individual is one person. Sometimes, "person" is even a synonym for "individual." But pathological data help us to become aware that the identity of persons (spirits, souls) and the identity of individuals are not based on the same principle. For instance, cases of amnesia show that we expect a person to recognize himself as the same individual through time. On the basis of factual information, we recognize an amnesiac as one individual before and after his accident, and yet he acts as if a new person had been born. In acute cases of schizophrenia, an individual may use two names, one for each personality. If we interpret a schizophrenic case as possession, we appeal to a principle of spiritual or personal identity clearly distinct from that of material individuation; one demonic spirit is assumed to be able to manifest itself in distinct individuals. A similar remark could be made about reincarnation, or shamanic telekinesis. Spirits behave like universals, but they are personified universals. Plato used "daemons" and a kind of discourse that he called "mythic" to provide a link between the world of historical individuals and the world of ideas.

The mystery in a mystery story is a narrative puzzle within a narrative development. The primary questions are "what," "who," "where," "when," and "how." The question "why" is ancillary. The investigative sequence sometimes stresses the question of motive, but it does so to draw the reader's attention away from the primary questions. The fictional detective may assert that the answer to the question of motive or purpose is decisive, and he may use a large dose of psychological explanations in his final narrative. But motives are means of personification rather than of individuation. Motives are not events. And the ascription of motives is bound to appear somewhat facile. One can always invoke some kind of madness or a desire to commit a perfect crime. After all, the function of the murderer in a detective-and-opponent story is to test the detective. Other motives are ornamental.

The basic objective of knowledge is historical determination. Science provides rules of individuation, process patterns to be used in order to determine what happened and what will happen. But cognition is irremediably uncertain and incomplete. If it were not, knowledge would eliminate the practical categories of decision and action. Causal necessity is only the limit of probability, and scientific rules are subject to verification, hence to disconfirmation.

Scientific or not, patterns of historical individuation are embedded in the meaning of words, and a language such as English offers the same vocabulary and syntax to both narrative fiction and historical reports. The mystery in a mystery story thus looks like a cognitive problem. But the way fiction uses rules of individuation is purely semantic, not cognitive. Unlike straight stories, hermeneutic tales keep the axiomatic character of fiction in suspense regarding some events. But they restore it fully at the end. More pointedly than straight stories, they show that narrative fiction projects the ideal of historical reports and predictions. The end (goal and result) of a hermeneutic tale is the end (ideal, inaccessible goal) of historical knowledge. From the standpoint of an "omniscient" god we would be fictional characters.

The epistemological significance of mystery stories is not to be denied. But to a great extent it should be viewed in a negative perspective. The same could be said about the significance of any esthetic experience compared to practical existence. Analogies, however realistic they may be, must not blind us to radical differences. Basically, art represents practical reality as it is not. It turns failures of comprehension into comprehension.

The differences between history and fiction are such that it may be wondered whether fictional characters, like historical entities, should be called individuals, hence whether it is appropriate to say that the mystery in a mystery story is concerned with individuation. I proposed continuity as a necessary but insufficient condition of individuality. A historical narrative may jump from Monday to Wednesday; while it describes what happens to an individual, it may say nothing about other individuals involved. But we assume that the gaps, in theory at least, could be filled by other narratives. In the case of a piece of fiction, on the other hand, filling gaps would amount to creating another fictional world. One of the differences between fictional individuals and "real" individuals is that a character cannot be assumed to exist outside what the text says about him. Does this not mean that characters who disappear and reappear behave like spirits rather than individuals? Does not fiction generalize the principle of reincarnation? And what about events beyond the span of a narrative? We assume that a human individual who is described only as an adult was a child. But the principle of fictional completeness does not allow the same postulate for an anthropomorphic character if nothing is said about his childhood.

The foregoing considerations are faulty insofar as they place fictional entities in a frame that has been borrowed from historical entities. Mapped against this frame, fictional processes, including the total process, will appear irremediably discontinuous. This procedure is countenanced by convenient, perhaps inevitable, turns of speech that incline us to picture location and duration together as an absolute receptacle, as an empty house to be furnished with events, which might be fictional instead of historical.

With some qualifications having to do with scale, this conception is all right when one deals with historical narratives; each narrative cannot be allowed to develop its own space-time. But, on the contrary, this is what fictionalizing narratives must be allowed to do. If a narrative is interpreted as history, the phrase "two days later" opens a hole which other narratives might fill. If the narrative is interpreted as fiction, the same phrase does not introduce a discontinuity any more than "and" in the sentence: "He stood up and began to speak." The spatio-temporal frame cannot be set apart from the peculiar way in which the processes are developed. The phrase "two days later" has a relational function, and relations, by themselves, do not open holes in the fabric.

The distinction between a conception of space and time befitting history and one befitting fiction is made difficult by the fact that the same topological and chrono-logical terms, among others, are used in both cases. It may be argued that even if the phrase "two days later" is bound by a fictionalizing operator, it still does not mean the same thing as "and then." No doubt it does not; the term's relational function does not eliminate whatever is implicit in the meaning of "two days." But the status of implicit meaning is not the same in narrative fiction as in historical reports. It is out of the question to propose a general theory of implicit meaning in fiction. Various texts, various styles mold it differently. I shall be content with a suggestion regarding phrases like "two days later." Let us think of the developed episode as present. It may be said that what is implicit in "two days" has the status of a present perfect that cannot be turned into a preterite. Similarly, it may be said that a human-like character who is solely presented as an adult has been, yet was not a child. This would agree with my use of the future perfect to define the goal of the narrated process in hermeneutic tales: "what will have happened." The denouement develops a preterite: "This is what happened." But as long as what is to be made explicit remains implicit, it is borne by a perfect modified by a future. One of Chandler's "Casual Notes on the Mystery Novel" even suggests a hermeneutic ending that would determine what is to be determined and yet that would manage not to make it flatly explicit: "The ideal denouement is the one in which everything is made clear in a brief flash of action." Artistically, this kind of denouement would be superior to explanations, however ingenious they may be. Implicitness provides esthetic meaning with a depth where inner resonances can play.

A refusal to call fictional characters "individuals" would be an appropriate decision if epistemological reality were equated with ontological foundation, hence if individuality were chosen as a basic category. Under these conditions only historical entities are "real" individuals; only they are really individuals. Instead of that, I take the position that individuals are the offspring of a certain logic, of an attempt to bring experience to reason, an attempt whose failure is sufficiently indicated by the fact that there are other logics and that narrative logic has a fictionalizing version. Fiction can serve to expose the ontological pretensions of history.

Possibility and impossibility

THE PROCESS PATTERNS embedded in the meaning of words that name classes of individuals delimit a range of narrative possibilities. What is epistemically impossible is impossible according to semantic conventions. If these conventions do not accommodate events that are recognized as having happened, they have to be revised. A piece of fiction may also explicitly modify the range of narrative possibilities. The introduction of fantastic elements has to be restricted; otherwise, narrative coherence would crumble, and the story would turn into a poem. The difficulty, perhaps the main purpose, of fantastic fiction lies in showing how a definite change affects the parts which abide by the conventions. There is a similar difficulty in philosophy: conceptualizing one word in a certain way affects the meanings of other words.

A story that resorts to fantastic ingredients may also have a hermeneutic aspect. For someone who is interested essentially in mystery stories and not in science fiction, this is not a promising hybrid. If the fantastic elements are carefully made clear, their delimitation will give the game away, or they will have nothing to do with the denouement, in which case they will appear superfluous. If, on the other hand, the alteration of narrative rules remains hazy, if it is not controlled, the denouement will appear gratuitous.

Some of the manifestations that are called "fantastic," "miraculous," or "supernatural" can be viewed as exceptions to customary process patterns. Others, which a culture codifies more or less precisely, concern persons rather than individuals. Spirits are not individuals. The business of a fictional detective is not that of an inquisitor. It does not consist of identifying demons and forcing them to sign confessions written in Latin or English.

Some mystery stories play with dual personalities. This device does not affect rules of individuation; rather, it stresses the difference between personal identity and individual identity. Its use is designed to fool a reader in search of a person instead of an individual. Dual personality is a variant of the disguise device.

Mystery stories develop variants and reflect on one another. Some texts manifest or incite a basic reflection on the genre. They are hermeneutic tales, but they add something which, while it does not belong to the genre, helps delimit it. *The Burning Court,* by John Dickson Carr, is one such text.

A descendant of the man who betrayed the Marquise de Brinvilliers, a well-known seventeenth-century poisoner, is poisoned. The character whose viewpoint is adopted is led to think that his wife, Marie, might be a reincarnation of the Marquise and also, for good measure, of a nineteenth-century poisoner. Another character, Gaudan Cross, puts him in mind of Gaudin St. Croix, the accomplice of the Marquise. There are two locked-room puzzles. According to a witness, a woman dressed like the Marquise has vanished through a wall of the victim's room, and the latter's body has disappeared from a crypt. The story ends with a solution that dispels reincarnation clouds, provides a murderer other than Marie, explains the vanishing act with the help of a mirror, and is buttressed by footnotes that refer the reader back to pages where corroboration can be found.

All of this is in Carr's usual manner. But his favorite detective, Doctor Fell, is absent; the solution is delivered by Gaudan Cross. And the denouement is followed by an epilogue that takes the form of an interior monologue attributed to Marie. Its content tends to confirm the reincarnation theme and vanishing trick and to identify Marie as the murderer (the presence of the infallible Fell would not have allowed this). A last chapter entitled "The Verdict" consists of a noncommittal quotation. The reader is left to do what he pleases with the two endings.

Actually, the epilogue does not provide a proper hermeneutic denouement. Reincarnation makes a difference to the conception of Marie as a person, not as an individual. What makes a difference to her individuality is the assumption that she murdered the man and somehow managed to "filter" through a wall. But this is not acceptable, because there has been no stipulation that, in her case, semantic limits of possibility were to be extended. A pseudotechnical explanation of what would materially occur during a transference from one side of a wall to the other should have been formulated in deference to the principle of continuity. However fanciful it might have been, the theory would at least have allowed Marie to remain one individual. She would have been a member of a class of individuals especially tailored for the occasion. If this had been done, there would have been two legitimate denouements. But both would have been disappointing, the first one because it would have made the special stipulation appear superfluous, the second because the stipulation would have disclosed it in advance. As it stands, the text shows what kind of denouement befits a mystery story in opposition to a kind that does not. If the reader is annoyed instead of amused by the epilogue, he can integrate it by assuming that Marie is crazy.

The reincarnation motif is similar to the dual personality device. But instead of two persons for one individual, it suggests one person for two individuals. In *D'entre les morts,* by Pierre Boileau and Thomas Narcejac, the reincarnation motif is adroitly exploited to draw the reader's attention away from an impersonation. A private detective is told by a client that the latter's wife is acting as if she were the reincarnation of a dead relative. But the woman whom the detective puts under surveillance is only acting as if she were the wife. A question relating to personality conceals a question relating to individuality.

Taking individuation for granted, novels in the nineteenth-century tradition can make personality their main topic. In opposition, the tendency of mystery stories is physicalistic. This tendency is similar to the main scientific trend. And there is more than a parallelism when physical and chemical tests furnish some of the fictional data. In the old days, a mastermind like Holmes even had to do the testing himself. But for fear of being dull, mystery story writers have generally avoided describing and explaining experiments at length. The narrative simply states the results of the experiments, or it makes them look like magic to an uninformed reader.

Scientific and technological progress modifies semantic conventions of possibility in ways that may interfere with the enjoyment of some mystery stories. If the solution to a narrative riddle relies on specialized scientific knowledge and fails to present this knowledge as a special semantic rule (for fear of giving the game away), this procedure will make the denouement appear unfair or disappointing if the reader is not independently acquainted with this semantic possibility. On the other hand, readers who are not experts will nowadays grant to electronic "miracles" a generous range of possibilities based on technical ignorance rather than knowledge. This will detract from the impression of impossibility that a story like *The Lost Gallows,* written by John Dickson Carr and published in 1931, attempts to produce. In the book a car seems to be driving by itself; today this would suggest the intervention of some remote-control device.

In their presentation of the data, some mystery stories try to convey an impression of narrative impossibility.[1] To achieve this appearance, the text may steer the reader's thoughts toward the wrong class of individuals. What seems impossible if we are led to think of normal adults may be within the range of children and dwarfs (this is the case in *The Lost Gallows*). What seems impossible in human terms may become possible if we think of an ape (as in Poe's *The Murders in the Rue Morgue*), a snake (as in Doyle's *The Speckled Band*), or a meteorite (as in Maurice Leblanc's *La Femme aux deux sourires*).

The change from dead to alive is a motif that has often been exploited, for instance by Poe in *Thou Art the Man* and by Boileau-Narcejac in *Au bois dormant.* In this motif, the impression of impossibility is based on a rule of irreversibility. Semantic conventions also forbid the metamorphosis from immobile to mobile object that is suggested in the title of a story by Edmund Crispin, *The Moving Toyshop.* Speed limits imposed on human individuals and means of transportation permit alibis to create an apparently impossible situation. Locked-room puzzles defy semantic rules bearing on solid objects. In such cases, the text takes care to eliminate the possibility of secret passages. In *To Wake the Dead,* Carr does resort to this notorious device in the denouement. But its relevance has been intimated cryptically, and if there is an appearance of impossibility, it has to do with the murderer, not with the whole situation.

One individual may be mistaken for two. In *Une Evasion d'Arsène Lupin,* by Leblanc, Lupin's Protean abilities allow him inexplicably to escape from jail. In *The Invisible Man,* by Chesterton, both the murderer and the victim manage to slip into a building whose entrance is being watched. Supposedly, it was enough for the murderer to masquerade as a postman with a big bag in order to pass unnoticed. The small size of the victim has been offered as a clue.

In daily practice we cannot track the trajectories of the individuals with which we are involved. We rely on a combination of lasting properties in order to identify them. And yet an individual is not, or is not just, a "bundle" of properties. Mystery stories play upon confusions between sameness of properties and individual identity, all the more easily since linguistic descriptions are more schematic than are perceptions or even memories. Natural resemblances are sometimes used as a pretext for describing two individuals as if they were one. Disguises may also serve this purpose as well as assisting in mistaking one individual for two. Two identical rooms are confused in *Le Monte-Charge,* by Frédéric Dard; in *La Demeure mystérieuse,* by Leblanc, there are two identical houses. In *Le Repos de Bacchus,* by Boileau, a painting seems to dematerialize and rematerialize elsewhere.

Whether the fiction resorts to disguises and forgeries or not, the appearance of impossibility, like other effects, depends primarily on descriptive style. It would be ineffective or disappointing to make it depend on lies. Deliberate misinformation is one of the most banal functions of practical speech. I consider it an artistic weakness to make the solution to a fictional mystery amount to an exposure of lies. It is a more interesting and esthetically sounder procedure to let an appearance of impossibility derive either from an honest error (that is to say, from the omission of an operator like "he thought he saw") or, even better, from a description that is not definitely invalid yet tends to lead the reader's thoughts away from the implicit meaning that the denouement will choose to develop.

Since in either case descriptions of events are supposed to formulate perceptual judgments of characters, the reader, when he has reached the denouement, may deem it unlikely that the character should have interpreted what he saw in the misleading way adopted in the description. If the solution to a locked-room puzzle appears to be a conjuring trick (a mirror illusion for instance) or a string-and-pin stratagem, the reader, whether he tests it or not, may find it unlikely that it should have worked. These remarks introduce the issue of probability.

Probability

IN VIEW OF the analogies between fictional mysteries and cognitive problems, it seems apposite to raise the traditional question of "probability," a term akin to "likelihood," "plausibility," or "credibility." Regarding situations, behavior of characters, and denouements, some theorists have insisted that mystery or detective fiction may be and even should be improbable. Others have taken the opposite view.[2] What can "credibility" mean when a narrative is accepted as neither true nor false? And what about "probability" or "likelihood"?

It is not a matter of mathematical probability. If a male character avails himself of a means of killing that, according to historical statistics, has been used by women nine times out of ten, no critic will deplore or applaud a lack of likelihood on this sole basis. Nor would any critic insist on having this particular method used nine times out of ten by female characters in the stories he happens to read.

The characters, incidents, or settings in a story may strike certain readers as strange compared to what they have been accustomed to in their practical lives, geographical locations, social and political environments. But this does not necessarily mean that these readers, unlike others, will interpret this oddness as improbability. Out of ignorance, they may instead assume that it is typical. Think, for instance, of a Frenchman reading a translation of Dashiell Hammett's *Red Harvest* without balanced information about small industrial towns in the United States in the 1920s.

A crime story that purports to be a faithful account of a historical case is expected to deal with a topic with some extraordinary features. Will this detract from credibility? On the contrary, the claim that what is going to be told is incredible is a rhetorical incitation to belief. The reader expects something extraordinary, so the extraordinary becomes normal. Certain kinds of improbability become probable with a certain kind of topic. In *A Catalogue of Crime,* Jacques Barzun and Wendell Hertig Taylor make this comment on a book that is characterized as the memoirs of a spy: "His adventures are of the usual unbelievable yet genuine kind."

The same goes for fiction. The situations, characters, and plot of a mystery story may appear improbable to a reader *if* he compares them with what he assumes to happen ordinarily in the historical field. This comparison will be encouraged by the deployment of a recognizable geographical, social, legal, or political setting, that is to say, by devices that may be called "realistic." But, on the other hand, as the reader becomes familiar with a certain type of content, with the habits of a particular author, resemblances between stories will constitute a kind of regularity, hence an increased "probability." One may thus reach the paradoxical conclusion that the most unlikely suspect should be the one picked by the solution and should thus be the most likely suspect for an experienced reader.

Like most promoters of literary schools, Chandler, in *The Simple Art of Murder*, adopts the battle cry of "realism." And he views the shift from the genteel to the hard-boiled manner as a gain in "plausibility." But, to take one main feature, are Spade and Marlowe more "plausible" than Poirot and Lord Peter? What is bothersome about texts that make a routine use of the conventions of a school of writing is not that they do not resemble "reality" but that they look too much like one another. The proper objective of a new writer is to introduce freshness, not more probability. If his way of writing becomes a fashion, an author's freshness is lost, and the probabilities instituted by literary routine may appear to some readers to mask what is historically probable. The hard-boiled manner adopts some habits of the genteel school (for instance, a successful detective) and generates some customs of its own. At the time Chandler wrote his short essay, these customs had already been set.

It should be noted, in this respect, that the order in which books are read by someone differs from the chronological order of publication. Suppose that a reader comes across *The Maltese Falcon* after reading several stories in which the murderer is a client who tries to seduce the detective. The fact that *The Maltese Falcon* exemplifies this pattern may disappoint him, not because he assumes that it is historically improbable (or probable) but because, in his eyes, the development of the story makes the denouement too likely. He may thus consider Hammett to be an imitator of authors who wrote after him. A historian of course can alter this perspective, but no historian, however learned he may be, can claim he has read all the mystery stories that have been published.

The trouble with critical judgments regarding probability is that they are apt to confuse three things: historical probabilities, resemblances between texts that establish kinds of regularities, and consonances between elements within one text. Esthetically, it is these consonances that matter, and, in this perspective, historical probabilities are irrelevant. Resemblances between texts are not devoid of relevance: readers will or should adjust their appreciation of consonances and dissonances according to whether they regard the text as a mystery story, a tragedy, an ontological essay, or a piece of science fiction. On the other hand, the particular text has to affirm its own consistency beyond genre conventions and routine arrangements.

Judgments of probability tend to divorce content from form. Remarks on internal consistency should reunite them. The same configuration of events may be recognized in two stories, but differences in formulation will make the configuration more acceptable in one case than in the other. Changes in style modify the relative weights of semantic possibilities. In his "Casual Notes," Chandler himself shows the pointlessness of his considerations on content alone when he says: "Plausibility is largely a matter of style. . . . Plausibility is a matter of effect, not of fact, and one writer will succeed with a pattern which in the hands of a lesser artist would just seem foolish."

Of course, the impression that the elements of a story

are well matched or not varies according to readers and even to reading and rereading experiences. A literary critic cannot "demonstrate" the consistency of a story; he can only endeavor to bring out the factors that are responsible for the impression of esthetic consistency or discrepancy he experienced the last time he read the text. Even if they agree on these factors, two readers may still honestly disagree as to the story's effect if they evaluate these factors differently.

Necessity

IT IS TEMPTING for a hermeneutic tale to move from an appearance of impossibility in the presentation of the enigma to an appearance of necessity in the presentation of the solution, thus going from one logical pole to the opposite. According to Chandler in his "Casual Notes," "the solution, once revealed, must seem to have been inevitable." "Seem to have been" and "inevitable" (instead of "necessary") are noteworthy qualifications.

A determination of historical events cannot close the gap between what must have happened and what did happen. What is accepted as true remains subject to verification. To varying degrees, the data are uncertain and incomplete. And the rules of individuation that are applied, even if they have scientific merit, may themselves be questioned. Some historical events are determined "beyond a reasonable doubt." But reasonable certainty is not synonymous with rational necessity.

Since fictional events are solely determined by words,

and by the words of one text, fictionalizing narratives automatically close the gap between events and their linguistic determinations. The semantic rules that the narrative adopts are not open to question. Since the data are invented, cannot the writer arrange them in such a way that the solution to the riddle will be rationally necessary rather than reasonably certain?

A definition offered by Régis Messac suggests this ambition. He defines a certain type of mystery story as "a narrative devoted above all to the methodical and gradual discovery, by rational means, of the exact circumstances of a mysterious event." This definition is reminiscent of the label that Poe proposed for his mystery stories: "Tales of ratiocination." It puts me in mind of denouements in which the detective adorns his sovereign decree regarding what happened with claims that no other solution is allowed (by semantic rules and the set of data), also of the "challenges to the reader" with which Ellery Queen prefaces the endings of some of his tales. But if "ratiocinative" is not synonymous with "reasonable," it is not synonymous with "rational," either. The ideal identity between cognitive induction and analytic deduction that a ratiocinative tale may project involves pseudoanalyticity as well as pseudocognitivity.

To convey an impression of analytic necessity, the denouement of a hermeneutic tale would have to be equivalent to a mathematical solution, derived from axioms (semantic rules) and hypotheses (data). But words are not mathematical symbols, and grammar is not a calculus. In this respect, the conditions of a mystery story are similar to those of a philosophical essay. The analogy would be particularly strong between ratiocinative hermeneutic tales and ratiocinative hermeneutic essays, the latter defined as essays that delineate a "problem," complacently emphasize difficulties (perhaps a baffling paradox), leisurely criticize solutions that have been proposed, and put an end to the conceptual suspense by presenting another solution as the only right one. Careful definitions and close reasoning tighten the overt fabric of essays. But outside obvious tautologies and simple syllogisms, philosophical conclusions do not necessarily follow from the premises in an analytic way. Spinoza's "geometric mode" is an artistic choice.

Like the conclusion of a hermeneutic essay, the denouement of a mystery story discloses something that had been left implicit. But the way in which the ending develops that "something" is not analytically entailed. To some extent, the solution given by story or essay is a new axiom. The difference, of course, is that a story develops some semantic possibilities narratively, whereas an essay develops them conceptually. The reader of a story cannot question narrative premises in the way the reader of an essay can object to definitions. But narrative premises can be questioned in another way; the reader can think of other possibilities on the basis of lies, honest errors, or ambiguous descriptions in the tale. Mystery stories alert the reader to such loopholes, especially when an appearance of impossibility is cultivated. An essay may accumulate definitions; a story may multiply clues. From the standpoint of analytic necessity, this strategy is of no avail. Each new axiom, definitional or narrative, brings new loopholes.

Parodies have not failed to make fun of the pretence of necessity, and pastiches of Holmesian inferences have been written. In *The Poisoned Chocolates Case,* by Anthony Berkeley, for example, six members of a detective club propose six solutions. Having listed twelve conditions, one of the members recognizes himself as the only individual who fulfills them all, and in concluding he must be the murderer he reflects: "Artistic proof is, like artistic anything else, simply a matter of selection. If you know what to put in and what to leave out, you can prove anything you like, quite conclusively." In the same text, the following remark is a reminder that the detective's solution is first of all a fictional fiat: "Nobody else is capable of drawing any deductions at all, and the ones he draws . . . are invariably right." In *The Face on the Cutting-Room Floor,* by Cameron McCabe, an epilogue points out that several characters could be made to fit the murderer's function, and it adds, with a good deal of exaggeration: "The possibilities for alternative endings to *any* detective story are *infinite.*"

The purpose of the foregoing paragraphs is the same as the remarks on probability. It is not to emphasize gratuitousness but to dispel a confusion between analytic necessity and the esthetic cogency of a narrative. In this perspective, a ratiocinative denouement should be interpreted as an oblique claim that the investigative sequence is composed in such a way as to make the chosen denouement the most appropriate esthetically. According to the reader's tastes and to the ratiocinative style, this device will be judged entertaining and exciting or heavy-handed and basically inapposite. It is to be noted that the appropriateness of a denouement concerns not only the way in which it makes narrative sense of the enigma but also its own status as final episode. I shall return to the topic of narrative cogency. Right now, I am interested in the relevance of narrative cogency to the guessing game.

In his "Casual Notes," Chandler decides that "it is not necessary or even desirable to fool to the hilt the real aficionado of mystery fiction. A half-guessed mystery is more intriguing than one in which the reader is entirely at sea. It ministers to the reader's self-esteem to have penetrated some of the fog. The essential is that there be a little fog left at the end for the author to blow away." This would apply to stories that conceal the mechanics of the murder as well as the murderer's identity. But ludic enjoyment depends on the reader as much as on the text. It depends on his reading experience, his familiarity with an author and with mystery stories in general. Above all, it depends on his tastes and moods. The judgments of critics of mystery stories are eminently diverse. On the subject of guessing as well as on others, I can only try to formulate my own reactions, to the extent that they have reached some stability.

In stories by Georges Simenon, *La Tête d'un Homme* for instance, Maigret is allowed to identify his opponent early. Certain details remain to be ascertained, but the interest in what will have happened does not detach itself from the interest in what will happen. On the other hand, in the case of texts that do stress a question of identity, the style and composition are sometimes such that I do not care which character the denouement will choose.

When I am incited to guess, I find that my appreciation of the ending has nothing to do with the rightness or wrongness of my surmises. I enjoy the bouquet of a denouement, but what matters above all is the "body," that is to say, the depth and comprehensiveness of the transfiguration. If I am incited to wonder, perhaps to guess, it is because the story appears to be oriented toward a potent denouement. The ending may not surprise me, it may surprise me pleasantly or unpleasantly. It may be better than the one I had projected, it may be as good, or it may be disappointing. In any case, I do not insist on being called upon to make a definite guess. Incitements to wonder are enough.

An investigative sequence that reliably and gradually discloses what is to be disclosed does not allow a strongly retroactive denouement. I prefer a stylistically "porous" development whose objective is to prepare the resonances of the ending. In order to be deep, the final transfiguration has to exploit some specific feature of narrative art. In this respect, the denouement of *The Murder of Roger Ackroyd,* by Agatha Christie, is especially noteworthy, since the chosen murderer is the character whose viewpoint has been adopted throughout. The allusion to this particular text in the title of Edmund Wilson's article "Who Cares Who Killed Roger Ackroyd?" suggests an insensitivity to narrative art as such. But, of course, if I happened to read a story whose pattern and style were strongly reminiscent of *The Murder of Roger Ackroyd,* I would be disappointed. And my critical estimate of Christie's story would be lowered if the other text had been published before. I should not be disappointed, however, if the same kind of denouement crowned a preparation that would be quite different yet as esthetically valid and appropriate.

When I read Christie's *Murder at the Vicarage,* I was led at first to think of a return pattern. Directly after the murder, a man and a woman make incompatible confessions. Solution: they are accomplices who try to protect themselves while appearing generously to protect each other. But as I was familiar with this pattern, I hoped the text would turn it into a "false" scent. The vicar's wife looked like a good alternate prospect, because she was the wife of a vicar and, more significantly, because the vicar was the narrator; she was, so to speak, narratively close to home. It would be nice, I thought, if the text let the reader suspect a complicity between the man and the woman who had confessed so as to cover a complicity between the man and the vicar's wife. But as I read on, the author seemed intent on making the wife more and more suspicious, while the picture of the two characters who had confessed was not significantly altered. So I returned to my original surmise. The ending confirmed it. It struck me as the right one not because I had happened to guess it but because it was the most appropriate under the circumstances. What disappointed me a bit was not the denouement but its preparation insofar as it chose to make another pattern less appropriate, a pattern that, on the basis of my reading experience, would have been fresher and, in view of the chosen narrator, more ironical.

Justice

MYSTERY STORIES often narrate the successful investigation of a crime. This does not necessarily mean that the characters who act as investigators are above suspicion; in *The Big Bow Mystery,* by Israel Zangwill, and in *Le Mystère de la Chambre Jaune,* by Gaston Leroux, the murderer is one of the detectives. Nor does it necessarily mean that the investigator is successful; the solution can be delivered by other means. Quite a few mystery story writers have kept the same investigating figure in several texts. The reader who is already familiar with Holmes, Poirot, Fell, Wimsey, Queen, Maigret, or Marlowe will take it for granted that he is dealing with a straight detective who will eventually succeed.

The conflict between detective and criminal and the "hoodwinking contest" between reader and text, both of which Carr in "The Grandest Game in the World" considers to be the main interests of this type of fiction, may be likened. The criminal, who furnishes problem and clues, is to the detective within the tale as the text is to the reader outside the tale. But this correspondence is limited. Whereas the detective is to succeed, the reader may make the wrong guess. Furthermore, the stylistic clues that the text offers to the reader have something to do with characters other than the murderer, the detective, for instance. The challenging behavior of the detective is apt to lead an unwary reader to adopt the wrong approach, to guess as if his position relative to the riddle were the same as the detective's. The two positions can be equated only if the data offered to the detective are contained in a text, quoted verbatim, and if the detective limits his activities to the presentation of the solution. This is the case in Boileau-Narcejac's *Au bois dormant.*

In most of the mystery stories I have read, the crime to be investigated, if there is one, is a murder, and many commentators proceed as if the detective-and-murderer pattern were the norm. In "The Art of the Detective Story," R. Austin Freeman considers that a murderer is an appropriate opponent for a detective, because "we want him to be a desperate player." Yet in quite a few stories, the murderer, once he has killed, is remarkably passive. Obstacles and threats can be thrown into the path of the detective by other means.

Death is a deeply resonant topic. To start living is to start dying, and living involves killing (plants, animals, humans). Death plays a part in every human experience as something to be feared or desired, delayed or sought, masked or exposed. Death has a practical and moral aspect (killing oneself or others); it also has an esthetic aspect. In a rather abstract and simplistic way, it alone allows one to view the life of an individual or of a species as a closed process. Practical activities set their goals beyond their spatiotemporal spans, but the goals of ludic and esthetic activities are immanent. When Montaigne wrote that death is the goal of our career, he effected (in words) an esthetic transposition by turning inevitable result into conscious purpose. So did Heidegger when he spoke of "being for death" and superimposed *Geschick* (destiny) on the cognitive notion of *Historie.* The same could be said about theological justifications of historical events and processes.

Most tragedies exploit the esthetic aspect of death. The connection of the motif with hermeneutic tales is looser; however, it does concern the detective-and-murderer pattern. It concerns not the fate of the victim, which is only a springboard, but the fate of the murderer, insofar as the latter has something to do with the goal of the investigation, and with reference to the fact that, in the countries where detective stories flourished, certain kinds of killing as defined by law incurred and may still incur the death penalty.

Some theorists have deemed it proper for a mystery story in which a crime is investigated to result not only in the identification but also in the punishment of the criminal.[3] And yet the crime-and-punishment pattern cannot provide the specific goal of a hermeneutic tale. Dostoyevsky's novel is not a mystery story. Besides, one may wonder whether punishment as an added goal does not interfere with the story's proper goal. A number of mystery story writers seem to have been bothered by this question. They find it convenient to exploit the ready-made detective-and-murderer pattern, but in various ways they attempt to avoid a confusion between this pattern and the crime-and-punishment schema.

The basic purpose of a *bona fide* detective—the only purpose that has something to do with the definition of hermeneutic stories—is to find out what happened. Other purposes are often added: the detective may seek financial gain; he may be after adventure, amorous for instance; he may want to protect himself, someone else, his country; he may seek vengeance. These various purposes are illustrated by Arsène Lupin. But Lupin is not a champion of the law. And other detectives, even though they are not rogues, are pointedly presented as not seeking punishment, legal or otherwise, for the criminal. In *Le Mystère de la Chambre Jaune,* Rouletabille makes this flamboyant declaration: "*I* have nothing to do with 'justice'. I do not belong to the police: I am a modest journalist and my job is not to apprehend people. . . . I serve truth as I see fit . . . this is my business . . . you defend society as best you can, that's *your* business. . . . I shall not be the one who brings a head to the executioner." In *Puissances du Roman,* Roger Caillois asserts, with some exaggeration, that "since Sherlock Holmes, the detective has been an esthete, if not an anarchist, not at all a guardian of morals and still less of legality."

The claim that the detective is not acting as a champion or minion of the law will appear somewhat hypocritical or immaterial if the result of his investigation is to bring a criminal to "justice."[4] Sometimes this is indeed what happens: the murderer is arrested, and we may even be told that he was ultimately sentenced to death. But in one way or another many detective-and-murderer stories manage to avoid this kind of denouement that, as far as hermeneutic tales are concerned, is superfluous if nothing else. In *Au bois dormant,* the events to be investigated happened more than a century ago. In the first part of *Les Dents du Tigre,* by Leblanc, and in *The Three Coffins,* by Carr, the murderer dies before he is detected. In *The*

Tragedy of Birlstone, by Doyle, the killing is recognized as self-defense. In *Le Mystère de la Chambre Jaune,* Rouletabille lets the murderer escape so as to enjoy a return bout in *Le Parfum de la Dame en Noir.* Lack of legal evidence may provide the detective with an excuse to let the murderer go scot-free; this is what occurs in *Five Little Pigs,* by Christie, and in *Chez les Flamands,* by Simenon. Quite often, the murderer is conveniently killed or kills himself at the end. In Simenon's *Pietr le Letton,* Maigret, though he is not a free-lance investigator, lends his pistol to the murderer. In most cases, the death of the murderer resembles euthanasia more than punishment. And it may even be interpreted as a way to stress his proper function. "Euthanasia" would then be given an esthetic rather than moral sense. A judgment of H. Douglas Thomson, in *Masters of Mystery,* suggests this transposition: "We expect the villain to make a 'good end'. He has been responsible for some share in our entertainment" and in the entertainment of the detective.

The mystery may be accidental, or it may stem from the behavior of characters other than the murderer. In stories that stress the murderer as the detective's hidden opponent, the murderer is a trickster: inside the fiction, he is the character mainly responsible for the riddle and the treacherous clues. In some tales, the detective's adversary issues a challenge prior to the murder as in *The Ten Teacups,* by Carter Dickson (alias John Dickson Carr); *A Murder is Announced,* by Christie; and *Crimes à vendre,* by Stanislas-André Steeman. Sometimes the author tries to purify the ludic approach by reducing to the utmost those elements of a murder that risk striking a reader as unpleasant. He pictures the victim as a disgusting character, or he invites the reader to look upon murder with "a dispassionate eye," as a "fait accompli" as Dorothy Sayers puts it in "Detective Fiction: Origins and Development."

The murderer is then comparable to the sphinx: his function is to concoct an enigma, and it is appropriate that he should die at the same time as the enigma. One of the differences between the two, however, is that the riddle proposed by the sphinx dealt with a class of individuals (man in general), whereas the detective in a hermeneutic tale is presented with a problem of individuation: the solution must be precisely narrative. In *The Blue Cross,* by Chesterton, a character likens the criminal to an artist and the detective to a critic. This is an apt metaphor if the fictional detective expatiates on the murderer's intentions and on the beauty or weaknesses of the murderer's scheme. Still, the basic mission of the detective is to make narrative sense out of the data. In this respect, he is a storyteller rather than a critic.

If the clues for which the murderer is responsible are devised in such a way as to impart a poetic charm to the mystery, the conflict between murderer and detective is a conflict between poet and storyteller. In this perspective, the detective's victory is a victory of narrative sense over poetic sense, or at least a superimposition of the former on the latter. The death of the murderer is the death of a poet. Will the reader applaud or deplore the fate of Orpheus? His reaction should be governed by the extent to which his tastes are oriented toward either narrative sense or poetic sense. In the latter case, he had better leave stories alone, whether they are mystery stories or not.

In a detective-and-murderer story, the identity of the murderer is part of the mystery, often its main part. As such, the murderer is not a person but simply an individual, that is to say, a composition of events. In this respect also, it is quite fitting that he should die at the end or be revealed as already dead. The detective's mission is to decide what will have happened. His solution does not dismember the murderer. On the contrary, it "members" him, composes him; but it constitutes him as past.

No more would have to be said about the ludic and esthetic transposition of murder and murderer if, in the practical field, murder were simply considered as a natural accident, one way among others in which death occurs, and the treatment of murderers as a social ritual. But murders are not simply a matter of biological, sociological, or psychological knowledge; they are also a matter of moral concern. How should a murderer be treated? This "should" may have at least three meanings: esthetic, legal, and moral. It is fine for mystery stories to distance their esthetic justice from the due process of law in a society. But the moral question is more ticklish; moral and esthetic aspirations should not be confused, yet they are not unrelated.

Under the label of "morality," socioreligious prescriptions are sometimes mistaken for moral principles. Coincidences do happen between moral fault according to someone's sensibility and judgment, sin according to some group, or crime according to some legislation. But this is no reason to equate good and evil with what is religiously or legally right and wrong.

Pain, not death, is what I consider evil. Pain is what prevents a sentient life, animal or human, from being lived under conditions of play. Coming too soon or too late, death, among other things, prevents a life from being a well-played game or series of games. But this is a lack of esthetic, not moral, value. The moral ideal leaves the quality of the game to esthetic appreciation. Death concerns moral sense insofar as, in one way or another, it involves suffering or puts an end to suffering.

The purpose of moral activities is to lessen the amount of pain. Since algometers have not yet been perfected, since the consequences of our actions cannot be evaluated with certainty and completeness, moral decisions remain *cas de conscience:* they are made in the dark, however clear the ideal may be. Still, what I take to be a properly moral attitude differs definitely from socioreligious poses which are still in vogue in our culture. It recognizes the fact that living is dying, that living involves either direct slaying or complicity, and that under certain circumstances inflicting death may be the lesser evil or represent no evil at all. Thus, this attitude would favor letting people commit suicide in the least unpleasant way, if they so wish.

In any case, from a moral standpoint penalties are to serve the purpose of prevention and deterrence, not expiation. Here as in other cases, a socioreligious mentality appears to confuse esthetic and moral values. Expiation for the sake of expiation looks like a means of achieving a kind of esthetic balance where it is pointless at best. The very label "justice" instead of, say, "collective safety," suggests the same confusion. Justice is an unconditional value only in the esthetic sphere. No doubt, it has something to do with my formulation of the moral ideal, according to which *every* experience should be lived under conditions of play. But it would function similarly in the definition of an immoral ideal: the greatest possible torture inflicted on each sentient being. And, in practice, to do some good somewhere is not to do any good elsewhere.

An esthete will verbally reduce evil to ugliness. Theologians are more ambitious: suffering is to be "justified" as part of the beauty of a divine novelistic plan. An opinion of Chesterton, in "A Defence of Detective Stories," can be used to illustrate a confusion between practical-moral and ludic-esthetic perspectives: "The romance of the police force is the whole romance of man. . . . The whole noiseless and unnoticeable police management by which we are ruled and protected is only a successful knight-errantry."

I have no misgivings about an esthetic transposition of death if it consists precisely of selecting and exploiting those aspects of the notion of death which are naturally esthetic in a poetic, fictional, or philosophical sense. As their basic concern lies in individuation, not personification, hermeneutic stories are apt to do this with more restraint and less fraudulent eloquence than will tragedies. The estheticization of pain is another matter. Since suffering to me makes moral antisense and esthetic nonsense, I am inclined to view its fictionalization as an imposture, whether it is done covertly (theologically, for instance) or overtly (in narrative fiction). No doubt, if a verbal fictionalization of pain helps a reader to fictionalize his own suffering, this is fine. But what about his attitude toward the pain of others, human or not, if they are incapable of the same conversion?

Of course, these considerations are purely theoretical. At present, there are no scientific means of estimating how a verbal fictionalization of pain is likely to influence the practical behavior of various readers under various circumstances. All I can do is play the philosophical game: distinguish between morals and esthetics, attempt to articulate them, and postulate that these operations are harmless at worst.

Most of the mystery stories I have read respect what might be called a rule of esthetic *bienséance.* Some of them tinge the narrative suspense with anxiety (a character who insists on being scared); few resort to descriptions of torture. On the whole, the main objective of the genre seems to have worked against obscene appeals to fear, pity, or sadistic voyeurism.

As far as murder and how to deal with murderers are concerned, it is not the job of a piece of fiction, hermeneutic or not, to make definite recommendations. Judgments voiced by characters sometimes provide hints,[5] but such suggestions are incidental. What is basic in a murderer-and-detective story is a ludic attitude toward murder and investigation. Shall we see in this fictional approach an encouragement to consider practical murder as "a fine art," according to Thomas de Quincey's phrase, or at least practical investigations as games? In most detective stories, fictional murder, investigation, and investigator are so bathed in "unreality" that the risk

of contamination appears slight. What a murder story
can do, on the other hand, is to use departures from
socioreligious imperatives and the substitution of esthetic justice for legal justice in such a way as to raise
moral questions implicitly, instead of spiriting them
away.

Trial and Error, by Anthony Berkeley, is a good example in this respect. Mr. Todhunter has just learned that
he has only a few more months to live. Without telling
his friends about this, he asks them what they think one
should do in this situation. To his surprise, they agree
that killing a particularly harmful individual would be the
right thing to do. Todhunter meets a woman who strikes
him as a good specimen of "pestilential nuisance." He
decides to kill her and apparently carries out his intention; he then adds a confession to his testament and goes
on a cruise. On his return, Todhunter learns that another man, Palmer, is to be tried for the murder. Todhunter accuses himself, but the police refuse to take him
seriously. Palmer is tried and sentenced to death. With
the help of an amateur detective, Chitterwick, and of Sir
Ernest, a barrister, Todhunter proceeds to build a case
against himself. Thanks to a peculiarity in the law, a
murder trial can be conducted officially with a civil party,
instead of the Crown, on the side of the prosecution;
thus Sir Ernest manages to have Todhunter convicted
and sentenced to death, much to the latter's relief. The
authorities are compelled to arrest him, so both Palmer
and Todhunter, though not confederates, are in the
same prison awaiting execution for one murder. Finally
Palmer is released. Todhunter dies of natural causes sec-

onds before the execution, and the last sentence of the text names the "real" murderer, whose identity it appears that Todhunter knew all along: "Mr. Chitterwick drew a deep breath of relief. Felicity Farroway's secret must surely be safe now."

Instead of a murderer acting as a detective in order to shield himself, *Trial and Error* proposes a would-be murderer acting as a detective in order to have himself convicted. The shuffling of means and ends contributes to a humorous treatment of the theme of punishment, of the legal ritual, and also of public opinion *(vox populi, vox dei)*. Todhunter's example shows how moral concern and decisions differ from socioreligious righteousness. His behavior is not exalted *ex cathedra* as a model that should be applied; the author has taken care to make his character amusing rather than impressive. On the whole, *Trial and Error* invites a metamoral reflection in a way appropriate to fiction.

People who hope to see "their" team win rather than a well-played game and who, after a game, declare "We won" though they never set foot on the playing field can hardly be said to adopt a properly ludic perspective. In a classical detective-and-opponent story, the detective's victory is one aspect of the denouement. But even if it adopts this pattern, a hermeneutic tale cannot be a straight hero vs. villain, we-against-them, story. Sometimes the character who triumphs is pictured as a mastermind, even a dashing hero. And inside the fiction, the hidden opponent is the Other. But if a reader approaches the text as a mystery story, he cannot "identify" with the detective. For, like other characters—the murderer in particular—the detective is a fictional adversary as much as a teammate for the reader.

From an esthetic standpoint, more may be asked. What should triumph is the text; it should achieve some artistic victory over linguistic difficulties. The triumph of a character within the fiction risks interfering with this perspective unless it corresponds to the artistic success of the text. It will be obtrusive if it looks like a practical success. It is not because they are rosy that "success stories" are unsuccessful stories.

Quite a few writers who adopt the detective-and-opponent pattern seem to have been aware of the snag. Unlike Erle Stanley Gardner, who stresses the worldly successes of Perry Mason, these writers have endeavored to reduce the investigator's victory to the success of the investigative sequence. Purposes other than investigative ones may be used to balance the character's success with failure. Private detectives often fail to make a penny, and the same goes for Lupin. Inside the fiction, the denouement may be tinged with sadness, disenchantment, or weariness; it may have the taste of ashes. Simenon does this for Maigret, Chandler for Marlowe. The following sentences are extracted from the last paragraphs of *The Big Sleep:* "What did it matter where you lay once you were dead? . . . You just slept the big sleep, not caring about the nastiness of how you died or where you fell. Me, I was part of the nastiness now. . . . On the way downtown, I stopped at a bar and had a couple of double Scotches. They didn't do me any good. All they did was make me think of Silver-Wig, and I never saw her again."

If the detective is to shine as a mastermind, it is

difficult to avoid the impression that he is trying to steal the show from the text as he displays his ingenuity in front of gaping stooges. Comic traits, which turn the mastermind into a crank or clown, have been used as palliatives. Thus we have the phony Gallic English of Poirot, his egg-shaped head, his mustache, his childish vanity. Such devices may be amusing; they may also be irritating.

It would seem that the reader is incited to identify with the detective if the latter is also the narrator. The fact that Marlowe is the fictional narrator in Chandler's long stories would seem to agree with this author's conception of the detective as expressed in *The Simple Art of Murder*: "He is the hero, he is everything." But Marlowe is not everything as hero (as detective); he is everything as narrator. And his successes or failures as a fictional narrator correspond exactly to the esthetic successes or weaknesses of the text. His role as total narrator extends the narrative mission of the detective. But he is not content to narrate; here and there, his reflections overshadow what is narrated, and his ironical remarks about himself detract from his possible status as a conventional hero. The trouble with this kind of technique may come from another quarter: why, when, and where is the fictional narrator writing, speaking, or simply remembering in the way he does? Unlike most critics, I do not think that the interpretation of any fictionalizing narrative necessarily involves the position of a narrator. But I would acknowledge that some narratives in the first person may constitute exceptions.

L'Aiguille Creuse, by Leblanc, illustrates another way

of preventing a hero from arrogating to himself the success that is due to the story: the tale projects antagonistic heroes. The narrative adopts the viewpoint of (although it is not narrated by) Beautrelet, a clever amateur who investigates a theft of pictures and the disappearance of a girl, Raymonde. It is clear to him that Lupin committed the theft and abducted Raymonde. To stop Beautrelet, Lupin, who is averse to killing, kidnaps Beautrelet's father. Beautrelet believes that Raymonde and his father are imprisoned in "the hollow needle," a place referred to in an otherwise undecoded cipher. As a matter of fact, he locates them in the "Castle of the Needle" in a district of France called *Creuse* ("hollow"). To free them, he enlists the help of the castle owner, Valméras, who subsequently marries Raymonde, with whom Lupin appears to have been in love. But old documents reveal that Beautrelet has not solved the mystery of the hollow needle. The needle was a state secret under the kings, and the castle was built to throw inquisitive people off the scent. Beautrelet eventually discovers that the cipher refers to a huge cone-shaped rock off the cliffs at Etretat in Normandy, which was hollowed out long ago and which Lupin is using as a warehouse and hideout. Beautrelet calls for police help to take over the needle. During the attack, he is cut off from the others and encounters Lupin, who expected him and whom he recognizes as Valméras. Thus Raymonde is Lupin's lawfully-wedded wife. Lupin escapes with Raymonde, taking Beautrelet along with them. But they encounter a private detective, who fires on Lupin and kills Raymonde instead. Beautrelet lets Lupin escape.

The text distributes success and failure between two heroes. Beautrelet deciphers the riddle, but Lupin had cracked the historic secret before him. Beautrelet finds Lupin's headquarters but does not capture him. Lupin had decided to abandon his criminal career anyway, for the sake of Raymonde, whom he has married with Beautrelet's blessing. But Raymonde is killed, and Lupin is thus prevented from retiring and can freely be launched into further adventures.

Part II / Story

Adventure

THE SOLUTION to the riddle determines some past events. But it is the development of an investigative sequence that makes a hermeneutic text a story as a whole. Query thus becomes quest; indicators of events (data, clues, denouement) are themselves indicated as fictional events. One aspect does not fully entail another; as suggested, for instance, by Dennis Wheatley's *File on Bolitho Blane* (British title: *Murder off Miami*), the items of a murder dossier could simply be given in juxtaposition.

Why should the set of data be turned into an investigative sequence? To allege verisimilitude would be irrelevant at best. What makes esthetic sense is that an investigative sequence can turn the opposition between narrative questions and answers into a tighter tension or complementarity between narrative progression and retrogression. This is implied in the phrase "what will have happened." Otherwise, the interplay between prospective and retrospective outlooks, predetermination and postdetermination would concern the reading process only. The fictionalization of the quest deepens the difference between the denouement and, say, the conclusion of a hermeneutic essay or the punch line of a poem.

A parade of witnesses or a summary of the results of an investigation delivered by a baffled police inspector to an armchair detective provide a rudimentary temporal sequence: one witness follows another, the inspector says one sentence after another. But quoted speech by itself yields fictional events of poor quality. Succession relies on simultaneity, hence on coincidences of diverse phenomena. Writers often take care to add notations on concomitant events to quotations of dialogues and monologues. But these insertions are apt to look too much like stage instructions. A storyteller cannot rely on actors, stage directors, and set designers to deploy a fictional space-time.

In "Detection and the Literary Art," Barzun considers the short story as "the true medium of detection." Indeed, if a reader of mystery fiction is interested in narrative art only to the extent that the riddle consists of narrative questions to be answered by the solution, he can be content with a perfunctory sequence to deliver the bundle of data. And if a short story is strong as mystery, I should acknowledge that it matters little if it is weak as story. But what about fairly long hermeneutic tales?

Some readers may prefer longer texts simply because they afford better means of concealment. Thus, the relation between two data can be hidden by distance: one may be situated on page 10, the other on page 100. R. Austin Freeman alludes to this factor: "The problem having been stated, the data for its solution are presented inconspicuously and in a sequence properly dislocated so as to conceal their connexion." Besides, a longer text can develop misleading scents. Detection then consists mainly of sifting, and the mystery may be likened to an experimental maze. But the fictional maze is not built of solid walls; blind alleys add loopholes.

To avoid an impression of gratuitousness, a longer text needs esthetic reinforcement. Narrative cogency can best justify what Freeman calls "dislocation," the distance between data to be connected, a delayed denouement, the development of misleading avenues. Though misleading, they can bear some relation to the chosen solution (analogy, contrast), and they can be integrated as events leading to the denouement as event.

In "On Detective Novels," Chesterton decides that "the *roman policier* should be on the model of the short story rather than the novel," because "the detective story is, after all, a drama of masks and not of faces" and thus cannot develop the psychology of characters. I should agree that a mystery story had better be shorter than *Madame Bovary.* But the reason would be that the text has to be precisely oriented toward the denouement, so its fabric must be tighter than those of leisurely nineteenth-century novels, regarding which it is often hopeless to try to discern what is padding and what is not. This judgment does not concern mystery stories in particular; it could be applied to any text whose cogency depends on narrative tightness. But this does not mean a preference for short stories. A fairly long text (a "novelette," or short novel) appears to me better suited than a short story to the deployment of a more-than-summary fictional process.

Chesterton's remark that a detective story is a drama of masks, not faces, may be derived from the principle that mystery fiction concentrates the interest on individuation, not personification. But this does not entail an elimination of psychology. Pure individuals are objects, but objectivity is correlative with subjectivity. The psychology that suits mystery fiction concerns the interpretation of signs as polysemic indicators of events. This kind of psychology is behavioristic if what is to be interpreted is the outward behavior of human characters. But the interpretation of what is perceived involves the psychology of the perceiver. Moreover, the text may very well project thoughts that are not directly related to perception. Without deviating from its purpose, a mystery story can even resort to the kind of psychology found in novels of atmosphere or novels of manners, if the creation of an atmosphere is to serve as a clue and the depiction of manners as a mask.

On the other hand, hermeneutic stories are by nature averse to the psychology that is characteristic of *romans d'analyse,* except, briefly, at the end, if the detective indulges in an analysis of the murderer. But it is to be noted that this kind of psychology is developed by means of summaries, free comments, set portraits, or reflective monologues—in a word, by devices that are not specifically narrative—so that the character is constructed as a set of properties rather than as a process. With Proust, the "analytic novel" veers to novelized analysis, becoming an essay that links its examples spatiotemporally.

In a mystery story, "human interest" and "local color" often look superfluous or merely decorative.[1] Some theorists have even banned "love interest." I would not go so far; love can serve as a motive or, better, as a mask. But I must confess that the treatment of love themes in some mystery stories is not only insipid, it is an artistic discrepancy.

To have narrative strength, a hermeneutic text has to be an adventure story in a broader sense than usual. By "adventure," I mean the power of a phenomenon as event, its "presence," its resonances in the spatiotemporal field. Adventure is opposed to routine insofar as routine muffles advent, absorbs it in generality. Adventure is a promise of destiny: the impression of adventure is to particular events what the impression of destiny is to the entire process. Adventure is to be enjoyed in itself; it fits a ludic and esthetic approach, not a practical and moral outlook. In Sartre's *La Nausée,* a character decides that "adventure is in books." But Sartre himself becomes a Romantic esthete when he characterizes history, limited to the human race, as "an adventure of nature."

As a rule, I should say that narrative strength is essential to fairly long hermeneutic stories. The case of *The Red Right Hand,* by Joel Townsley Rogers, which will be analyzed later, is rather special. It presents a lengthy interior monologue that accumulates the data in a series of dislocated evocations. The episodes are pictured quite vividly, but when the story is read for the first time, I doubt that the series can coalesce into a clear spatiotemporal sequence. This technique may be viewed as an attempt to adapt a structure that is good enough for a short story to a fairly long text. Unlike others, this particular attempt struck me as esthetically successful. But *The Red Right Hand* is a borderline case. It is only on second or third reading that it can be fully appreciated as a mystery story or as a comprehensive parody.

Viewpoint

THE AUTHOR and the reader of a piece of narrative fiction are historical individuals. They are not situated in the same field as the events that are narrated. In the fictional field itself there may be characters who narrate, such as, in a mystery story, the witnesses and the detective at the end. Sometimes there is even a character who functions as primary narrator from beginning to end. In this case, the whole text becomes dual. A basic narrative without quotation marks indicates a fictional narrator. His report is an exact replica of the basic narrative. But, unlike the basic narrative, it is an event or process in the fictional world, it is implicitly bound by quotation marks. Critics have often failed to distinguish between the basic narration and the words of the fictional narrator. Furthermore, influenced by the fact that a historical report is to be attributed to a historical reporter, they have automatically supplied a mythical narrator when the text does not posit a fictional narrator. They have transferred the cosmological argument (a clock implies a clockmaker) from metaphysics to narrative fiction.

A narrative can project the viewpoint of a character without implying that he uses words. The fictional viewpoint can be carried by a character who is shown to be perceiving, acting, imagining, remembering, or cogitating without words. Strictly speaking, such a character is an observer or an experiencer, not a narrator. Narratives written in past tense and in the first person seem to posit a character who uses words. But quite often the fictional time and place of his narrative activity are not precisely indicated, and it is not even made clear whether he is writing, speaking, or simply remembering. I shall not discuss the questions that are raised by this evasive procedure. What matters for my analysis is the identification of the character who carries the fictional viewpoint and the difference between a primary viewpoint posterior to the denouement, whether the character is assumed to use words or simply remember, and a primary viewpoint that is not posterior to the denouement. The latter does not necessarily mean that the inscription of the viewpoint is simultaneous with the described events; the character may be shown to remember or write a diary instead of simply perceiving.

The fictional viewpoint situates inner and outer events in relation to one another. If the carrier of the viewpoint remembers, the two kinds of events (remembered and remembering) are widely separated in time and possibly in space. If the narrative indicates a perception, the temporal separation disappears. The spatial distance also disappears if the story describes the feelings and actions of a character from his own viewpoint.

It should be noted that, by itself, a narrative in the third person and in a past tense does not add memories to perceptions.

Characters who carry the viewpoint are open characters. Some narratives use several open characters, and the viewpoint jumps from one to another. But there should be at least one open character at all times; the position of a fictional object implies the position of a fictional subject. This principle does not exclude strictly behavioristic narratives. A character is minimally yet sufficiently open if he can be assumed to observe his own behavior in the way it is described. If he is unconscious, another character has to observe his behavior.

However, in many texts traditionally labeled "novels," there are passages that do not project what a character thinks and experiences at a certain time in the fictional field. Such passages have been called "authorial intrusions." Since the author, after all, is presumed to have written the whole book, the label, though usually innocuous, is inappropriate. Thus I shall refer to these "intrusions" as "free" or "unattributed" comments. These comments may take the form of philosophical opinions about the way things are or the way people behave, opinions that cannot be attributed to any character at any time. Descriptions of settings, physical and psychological portraits of characters, summaries of their past, and serious or ironical judgments ("this admirable woman") may similarly be devoid of any connection with what a character is assumed to be thinking or observing at a certain time. Free comments become somewhat cynical when they explicitly resort to the device of the nonexistent observer: "If a keen observer of human nature had passed by, he would have noticed. . . ."

Are free comments esthetic flaws? It depends, of course, on the tastes of the reader, and it depends also on the perspective of interpretation and appreciation that best fits the text. What may be said in general is that such passages, while they may be interesting and amusing in themselves, are extraneous elements if the text as a whole is expected to create a closed fictional world. Of course, one may adopt a different global perspective. But it is with narrative art, more precisely with the handling of fictional viewpoints, that I am concerned.

The physical situation of fictional characters is irrelevant to philosophical or poetic technique. For instance, the first-person pronoun is mostly used in this essay to mark a philosophical position, not a spatiotemporal location. The cinema and the theater, which are not basically linguistic arts, turn the device of the nonexistent observer into a principle. The spectators who attend a theatrical performance are the real observers of real actors and props. But they have to discount their physical situation in order to project characters in the fictional world of the performed drama. In a film, the camera carries the viewpoint. But if the film is to be interpreted as fiction, not as a documentary, the physical situation of the camera and of the cameraman must be discounted. In the film *The Lady in the Lake,* adapted from Chandler's book, the "eye" of the camera is made to coincide with that of Marlowe. But instead of subordinating the camera's viewpoint to a character's viewpoint, the result is to disembody the latter. This technique clearly shows that a camera does not see as an incarnated person is supposed to see, because, first of all, a camera can only "see." It cannot by itself provide the means of distinguishing between, say, a hand moving, my hand moving involuntarily, or my hand moving voluntarily. Words, on the contrary, can do this quite economically.

Mystery stories alert the reader to the importance of the fictional viewpoint. Authors have to be particularly careful in the choice of observers, measuring their degree of openness, blending their reliability and unreliability in such a way that the reader may be hoodwinked and yet not cry "Foul!" at the end. The question of the viewpoint has emerged in the twentieth century as one of the main topics for critics interested in narrative art. But in his comments on *Barnaby Rudge,* Poe had already raised the question, and to do this he adopted the attitude of a reader of mystery stories, in connection with the concealment of the identity of a murdered character: "When, at page 16, we read that 'the body of poor Mr. Rudge, the steward, was found' months after the outrage, etc., we see that Mr. Dickens has been guilty of no misdemeanor against Art in stating what was not the fact, since the falsehood is put into the mouth of Solomon Daisy, and given merely as the impression of the individual and of the public. . . . The case is different, however, when Mrs. Rudge is repeatedly denominated 'the widow'. It is the author who, himself, frequently so terms her."[2] In my terminology, "the widow" would be a free comment. In a straight story, this stylistic device might escape notice; it would be one way, among others, of proffering axioms. But a reader of mystery stories is intent on distinguishing clear and valid axioms from axioms that are invalid and from those that are valid but ambiguous. Since it cannot be attributed to a mistaken or lying character, a free comment should provide the reader with a valid axiom. But in the case of "the widow," the axiom is invalid. For a reader of mystery stories, this constitutes foul play.

Mystery story writers have been led to be more chary of unattributed comments than were straight novelists who were their contemporaries. In this respect, they may have exerted an influence on narrative technique in general: free comments become rarer in the twentieth century. This does not mean, however, that this device is completely absent from mystery stories. Sometimes it has nothing to do with the guessing game, as in descriptions of settings. Sometimes free comments set valid but ambiguous axioms. But there are also cases similar to the "misdemeanor" scored by Poe.

The Seven Dials Mystery, by Christie, sets up no narrator. The fictional viewpoint jumps from one character to another. It is shared, in particular, by three characters: Bundle, Jimmy, and Loraine. The reader is incited to form the impression that the three enjoy the same status and that, since Bundle is obviously innocent, the same goes for Jimmy and Loraine. He may fail to notice that these two characters are less open than Bundle.

The trickery is reinforced by some free comments. Thus, Jimmy is said to be "a healthy young man with a natural dislike to being reminded of death." A reader who would take it for granted that a murderer cannot be said to be healthy would mistake this comment for a categorical assertion that the death in question cannot be Jimmy's work. Consider also this passage: "Now it may be said at once that in the foregoing conversation each one of the three participants had, as it were, held something in reserve." This warning is counteracted by the fact that it bears equally on Bundle, Jimmy, and Loraine. A reader who is not used to Christie's stratagems may fail to notice that, while what Bundle held in reserve is quickly made clear in the following pages, the same procedure is not followed for Jimmy and Loraine.

The device of the nonexistent observer is used at least twice in connection with Loraine. It is quite explicit in this passage: "And yet, if you studied the girl's face, you saw that there was strength of purpose in the small, resolute jaw and the lips that closed it together so firmly." Since the behavior of Loraine has not been pictured as irresolute, the passage does not seem to provide a clue. What is suspicious is, at most, the fact that the text resorts suddenly and superfluously to a nonexistent observer. Another passage raises a question: "Still Loraine ran—blindly, as though panic-stricken—right round the corner of the terrace—and slap into the arms of a large, solidly built man." How is "as though" to be construed? Loraine, who is carrying stolen documents, will pretend that she was not the intended receiver and that, if she ran away with them, it was because she was afraid an unknown villain might catch up with her. Does she want to convey this impression as she is running, in which case "as though" would legitimately conceal "wanting to appear"? No, since she is not observed and does not think she is observed, except at the last moment when she has rounded the corner and runs into the solidly built man, who is a police inspector. Does "as though panic-stricken" indicate the thoughts of the inspector? No, since it will be made clear that he is not deceived and since, in any case, he cannot have observed her before she rounded the corner. So the phrase "as though panic-stricken" must allude to the impression that a nonexistent observer would have received. But the text avoids saying something like: "she ran in a way which, had she been observed, would have conveyed an impression of panic." Is the phrase "as though panic-stricken" an unfair misdirection? In such cases, which occur fairly often in hermeneutic stories, it is as difficult to make a decision as in sports, for instance when one has to judge whether a tennis player set foot inside the serving line before hitting his service. Acting as a self-appointed referee, I should decide that "as though panic-stricken" is indeed a fault.

In the first pages of *Les Quatre Vipères,* by Pierre Véry, the narrative, written in the third person, adopts the viewpoint of Claude Beaumont as he finds a treasure worth millions in an African jungle. Then it is revealed that he is only daydreaming: "Millions. At that moment, close to his ear, the voice of a young girl. . . ." This is still his viewpoint; without a transition, yet unequivocally, the text has turned from what he dreams to what he perceives. Then the text resorts to free comments: "Every day, Claude Beaumont dreamed he found a treasure." General information is given about him, followed by this summary: "Such was Beaumont. A dreamer." This is the main clue. Beaumont is going to dream that he is temporarily mistaken for an accomplice by Moura, a member of a picturesque and sinister gang. He will write his dream as a factual report for a newspaper, and he will carry on as a reporter when what is taken to be the signature of the gang, a snake-shaped vial, makes its appearance on the scene of a crime.

The first pages of the book are so candid that they threaten to make it impossible for any reader to be fooled. Beaumont has been characterized as a dreamer. Furthermore, the text has shown that a description of events from Beaumont's standpoint is not to be taken as stylistic proof that these events are perceived or remembered rather than dreamed. But Beaumont's report is corroborated by the fact that crimes indeed will be committed. They are not narrated from Beaumont's standpoint and they are linked to his story by the discovery of the peculiar vials and by appearances of "Moura." It will be revealed at the end that Beaumont provided these vials and that a friend of his, Mrs. Durban, played the part of Moura in the crimes. Beaumont acts overtly as an amateur detective and covertly as a somewhat passive accomplice of his enterprising friend. This situation allows the following presentation of his thoughts: "Miss Bourgeois did not kill. It was Moura. It has to be Moura . . . until then she had stolen . . . only stolen." In his mind, Mrs. Durban has become confused with Moura, the character he dreamed up, and he did not expect her to go as far as to kill.

But I am uneasy about a comment that, in the first chapter, is designed to support Beaumont's original story, before any crime is committed: "It was this moment that Adventure chose to present itself and pull him away from the daily routine which despaired him. The fact took place in the narrow and shabby Rue de la Huchette." The first sentence can be justified. The reader has just been warned that Beaumont is an inveterate dreamer, and the sentence can be interpreted as a free comment bearing on the whole plot. In view of its unforeseen repercussions, what Beaumont is going to dream will become a "real" adventure, quite different from his usual evanescent dreams. But the phrase "the fact took place" cannot be made to cover these repercussions. Since it alludes only to the beginning of a pure fabrication, it is an unfairly invalid comment. Later on, when Beaumont pretends to meet Mrs. Durban for the first time, a comment is made upon the "deep and sudden" impression that she makes upon him. Since this comment is not attributed to an innocent bystander, I consider it also to be a stylistic fault.

The Valley of Fear, by Doyle, is curiously assembled. In the first part, *The Tragedy of Birlstone,* which takes place in England, Watson, who participates in the investigation, carries the viewpoint. The second part, entitled *The Scowrers,* which unfolds in America, is concerned with previous events that explain those narrated in the first part. Watson no longer carries the viewpoint; he was not present when these earlier events took place, and the story goes far beyond whatever information he might have gleaned. To some extent, the story adopts the perspective of McMurdo, a Pinkerton agent who manages to infiltrate a gang. But there are also free comments. The device of the nonexistent observer, for instance, is explicitly used at one point: "The man who studied him more closely might discern a certain firmness of jaw and grim tightness about the lips which would warn him that there were depths beyond." This can pass for a fair warning to the reader. But consider this other passage: "McMurdo's criminal soul seemed to have already absorbed the spirit of the vile association of which he was now a member." This unattributed comment would be valid only if "seemed" qualified "criminal soul" as well as the rest of the sentence.

A behavioristic style favors a parallel between narratives and films. This parallel suggests the elimination of a certain kind of free comment: summaries of the past, categorical judgments. It also suggests a generalized reduction in the degree of openness, a reduction that agrees with the aims of mystery story writers. On the other hand, it should be remembered that the camera is a nonexistent observer. What is shown in a film may correspond roughly to what fictional characters observe in a story, but it may also correspond to a free comment.

The Maltese Falcon is written in the third person. On the whole, it adopts the viewpoint of Spade as an observer, not as a narrator. But on the first page there is a physical sketch of Spade and of his secretary. No doubt they are together at that time and can observe each other. But since this is far from being their first meeting, can they be assumed to be reflecting on each other's anatomy, or on their own? Spade is described again in another passage: "He took off his pajamas. The smooth thickness of his arms, legs, and body, the sag of his big rounded shoulders, made his body look like a bear's."

Nothing allows us to presume that Spade, who is alone, is commenting inwardly on his physique at that particular time. But while such passages raise an issue regarding narrative art in general, they have nothing to do with the denouement.

A text that narrates events in the first person and in a past tense adopts the viewpoint of the character designated by the first-person pronoun at the time he reminisces, with or without words. This technique has the advantage of automatically binding what would otherwise be free comments. Thus, in Chandler's Marlowe stories, the reflections with which the narration is laced can be attributed to Marlowe. In Doyle's stories, the physical and psychological sketches of Holmes and Watson can be attributed to Watson.

Normally, the point of view in the past is basically carried by the first-person character; events are described as he perceived them. Sometimes, however, the story narrates events that the first-person character did not perceive. The text then adopts the fictional viewpoint of a third-person character. This is a potential source of trouble. The text is apt to forget to indicate how the first-person character became acquainted with events that took place in his absence, to what extent he reports a testimony, and to what extent he imagines and decorates. As already noted, the second part of *The Valley of Fear* goes further; Watson's mediation is eliminated.

In a straight narrative, narrating ego and narrated ego normally share the same degree of openness. The narrating ego may intervene in the description of a situation so as to provide more information or insight than is granted to the narrated ego: "At the time, I did not realize that George was lying." This kind of intervention may also occur in a mystery story, but on the whole, the requirements of concealment prevent the narrating ego from broadening the perspective allowed to the narrated ego. This means that the narrating ego is more secretive if he is assumed to be acquainted with the whole sequence of events, a privilege that the narrated ego can enjoy only at the end of the story. This difference in openness may be reduced in two ways: the narrator may be presented as writing a diary, or, at some point before the denouement, an illumination is said to take place ("Suddenly I knew"). If the narrated ego then does not enlighten other characters at once, he becomes as secretive as the narrating ego. This kind of announcement is a challenge to the reader; it is time for him to place his bet.

Narrating ego and narrated ego are one and the same character, yet their viewpoints differ. This ambiguity is a source of legitimate trickery. The narrated ego is permitted to lie, be mistaken, change his mind. If the narrating ego is situated after the denouement, he is not entitled to lies, errors, or contradictions since he is the fictional projection of the basic narrative as a whole. The statements that are attributed to him must be valid axioms. The text can try to trick the reader by letting him attribute to the narrating ego what need only be attributed to the narrated ego. But if the author is not careful, the kind of unfair misdirection already noted in connection with free comments is liable to occur.

The fictional historiographer of Arsène Lupin participates briefly in the events narrated in *L'Aiguille Creuse*. But, apart from this episode, the story is told in the third person and mostly adopts the viewpoint of Beautrelet, the amateur detective. This is somewhat troublesome, since the first-person character is not presented as Beautrelet's confidant. Still more troublesome are several passages concerned with Lupin masquerading as Valméras. Lupin-Valméras helps Beautrelet to free Raymonde from Lupin. He is thus able to marry her officially. Raymonde herself, in love with Lupin, contributes to the deception. But consider this passage: "What amazed Beautrelet and Valméras more than anything else was the disappearance of the wounded man." As Valméras, Lupin has only pretended to knife one of his own men. The sentence thus offers a clue to the reader. But from whose viewpoint can Valméras be said to be amazed at the disappearance of Lupin's accomplice? It cannot be his own viewpoint, since he is Lupin. In Beautrelet's presence, he pretends to be amazed. But this particular sentence does not privilege Beautrelet's standpoint; it puts "Beautrelet" and "Valméras" on the same grammatical footing. Nor can the sentence project the viewpoint of the historiographer as a deceived observer; he was not present. It is as narrator that he has to endorse the statement, as a narrator who is not a diarist and who knows that Valméras is Lupin. So the assertion is an illegitimate misdirection. The same could be said about this other statement: "Valméras fell in love with the melancholy charm of Raymonde." This was indeed what happened to Lupin. But as Valméras, he could only pretend to fall in love with a woman whom he already loved.

The following excerpt from *Thou Art the Man*, by Poe, calls for a different analysis: "Well, on the Sunday morning in question, when it came to be fairly understood that Mr. Shuttleworthy had met with foul play, I never saw anyone so profoundly affected as 'Old Charley Goodfellow'." Goodfellow is the murderer; the first-person character acts as detective. One could not justify the statement by saying that "saw" simply shows that the detective was deceived at the time, since he will assert that he suspected Goodfellow from the start. But while the story does not play on the duality between narrated ego and narrating ego, it exploits the duality between the first-person character's view of Goodfellow and that of the deceived villagers, the latter view being adopted partly in an ironical fashion. The name "Goodfellow" and the nickname "Old Charley" are already ironical. In the quoted passage, the irony is stressed by the use of quotation marks. They make the following interpretation possible: I could see that the Goodfellow whom the villagers trusted was profoundly affected, but in my eyes, this Goodfellow was only a mask; I suspected that without quotation marks Goodfellow might be a bad fellow and that, if he was affected, it might be not because Shuttleworthy had met with foul play but because Shuttleworthy's wounded horse had managed to come back, contrary to Goodfellow's expectations.

Another passage is more troublesome: "As if to demonstrate beyond a question the guilt of the accused, Mr.

Goodfellow, after considerable searching in the cavity of the chest, was enabled to detect and pull forth a bullet of very extraordinary size, which, upon trial, was found to be exactly adapted to the bore of Mr. Pennyfeather's rifle, while it was far too large for that of any other person in the borough or its vicinity." This time, there are no ironical quotation marks and "Old Charley" disappears. "Was enabled to detect" seems to assert a "fact" guaranteed by the first-person character. To defend Poe against the charge of a "misdemeanor against art," one would have to claim that an ironical ambiguity regarding the primary viewpoint has already been established in such a way that it may be assumed to contaminate the passage. And it could be argued that, on this basis, the phrase "as if to demonstrate" constitutes a sufficient warning.

Thou Art the Man makes one aware of the trouble which is apt to arise from a basic ironical tone: its power cannot easily be controlled. Commentators of venerable texts have tried to justify what is objectionable (silly, shallow, unfashionably prejudiced) by saying that it is ironical. This tactic cannot be applied to mystery stories. If the reader adopts the principle that irony may freely pervade moral and psychological judgments, what prevents it from freely contaminating statements of physical facts? The way in which *Thou Art the Man* is written does not encourage the reader to take this step. But it does extend the power of the irony over sentences where it is not clearly in evidence. Thus it shows the danger.

One of the prescriptions in Ronald Knox's detective story decalogue enjoins aspiring Watsons (*i. e.,* fictional narrators) not to be secretive. But while a Watson may be candid as a narrated character, he conceals what he knows as he narrates. The Watson-Holmes approach allows the thoughts of the detective to be part of the riddle. But letting the detective himself carry the primary point of view in the first person (Chandler's Marlowe) or in the third (Simenon's Maigret) does not necessarily involve more objectionable means of concealment.[3] What matters is a certain consistency in the degree or mode of openness.

A strictly behavioristic style reduces carriers of the viewpoint—the detective for instance—to observers of outward events, including their own actions. Instead of this, a narrative may reveal the reflections of the detective in certain respects but may avoid mentioning what he is planning and what he is thinking about the riddle. In this case, an announcement that the detective is enlightened at last could be considered a stylistic inconsistency. But it would not be more irritating than some of the sibylline remarks and flimsy pretexts for secrecy that detectives like Holmes, Poirot, or Doctor Fell inflict on their long-suffering recording angels.

In *The Murder of Roger Ackroyd,* the first-person character, Doctor Sheppard, who carries the primary viewpoint throughout, is the murderer. He lies as a witness, but as a narrator, he must not and does not lie. Since he is a diarist, he could be mistaken; he could be, for instance, an unconscious murderer. But the text does not avail itself of this possibility. It relies instead on ambiguity and evasiveness. Sheppard hoped to be able to record a failure of Hercule Poirot without accusing himself. At the end, before killing himself, he can take pride only in his tricky style:

> I am rather pleased with myself as a writer. What could be neater, for instance, than the following: "The letters were brought in at twenty minutes to nine. It was just on ten minutes to nine when I left him, the letter still unread. I hesitated with my hand on the door handle, looking back and wondering if there was anything I had left undone." All true, you see. But suppose I had put a row of stars after the first sentence! Would somebody then have wondered what exactly happened in that blank ten minutes?

What is, perhaps, not so neat is the way Agatha Christie uses her character to justify and congratulate herself.

At one point, Poirot says that he adopts the attitude that anyone may be lying. And he adds: "You, for instance, Doctor Sheppard." But he proceeds to show that some of Sheppard's statements are corroborated by other witnesses. In fact, it is as primary narrator that Sheppard does not lie, on a semantic plane where he can be corroborated only by himself; his "truthfulness" is the fictional image of the coherence of the basic narrative. On this plane he can afford to state, without giving himself away, that he lied to his sister: "I had to make up a slightly fictitious account of the evening in order to satisfy her, and I had an uneasy feeling that she saw through the transparent device." The clue is veiled by the presentation of the sister as a gossip, to whom Sheppard usually tries to give as little fuel as possible.

A Kiss before Dying, by Ira Levin, adopts the viewpoints

of several third-person characters. The first part uses the viewpoint of the murderer exclusively. The planning of the murder and the murder itself are described without ambiguity, but the murderer's name is not given. The second part shifts to the viewpoint of Ellen, a sister of the victim, Dorothy. Acting as an investigator, Ellen manages to guess what was revealed to the reader in the first part. She decides that the murderer must have been a boyfriend of Dorothy, but her suspicions fasten on the wrong man. The murderer is the character who has become Ellen's own boyfriend. He kills her, too. It is at this point, about halfway through the book, that the name of the murderer is disclosed. For a reader of mystery stories, it is a pity; the concealment could easily have been carried further. Nevertheless, *A Kiss before Dying* strikingly illustrates the fact that a story can elegantly conceal the identity of a character while adopting his viewpoint in quite an open and direct manner.

The Horizontal Man, by Helen Eustis, also shifts the viewpoint from one character to another. The thoughts of various characters are indicated, including those of the murderer. But the murderer is a psychotic with a dual personality: his normal persona is that of George Hungerford, his abnormal persona is feminine. As George, he is unconscious of the murder that he committed when he became possessed by his other persona, "Eloise." And he does not realize that, as Eloise, he writes the mysterious notes that appear in his apartment. The reader may suspect another character, Molly, of being their author. As Eloise, Hungerford switches to a falsetto voice that is overheard by his neighbor, Leonard, and that recalls the voice of still another character, Freda. Leonard himself is a possible suspect: like those of Hungerford and Molly, his thoughts, as revealed to the reader, spell psychological trouble. Some mystery stories simply rely on the assumption that several witnesses may be lying to the investigator. The situation is similar in *The Horizontal Man,* but this time the characters may be lying to themselves. In either form, this lying tactic by itself has the unfortunate result of making the chosen solution no more appropriate than another.

As in *A Kiss before Dying,* the actual murder is described in *The Horizontal Man,* and the use of a pronoun instead of a name allows the identity of the murderer to remain hidden. But this time, the pronoun also conceals the fact that the murderer, George Hungerford, is male:

> "No!" she cried, loud and harsh—and it gave him hope that someone might hear that voice—"I'm not sick! At last I am well, at last I can tell you, Kevin! My God, do you know that it is like water running down my dry throat to say that I love you?" His hand gripped the mantel; slowly, and—he hoped—imperceptibly, he began to edge toward the door. But her eye saw everything; she took a step toward him. "You can't stop me!" she triumphed. "*He* can't stop me! I'm free at last once and for all, and I tell you I will have you, Kevin, we can be together at last, rid of him!"

Hungerford-Eloise says "he" to refer to George Hungerford. Outside the quotation marks, the feminine pronoun indicates Eloise. The trick would be fair if Hungerford-Eloise carried the primary viewpoint during the scene. This is not the case. The primary viewpoint is carried by the victim, Kevin. From Kevin's standpoint, Hungerford may appear possessed by a feminine *persona,* but he still should remain a male *individual.* In this respect, unlike the pronoun "she," the neutral expression "that voice" is unobjectionable.

Most often, errors in the interpretation of what a character sees are explained by the fact that someone was disguised, that another witness made a misleading statement, or by a conjuring trick. But they can also occur without this kind of help; the observation may take place under poor conditions (bad lighting, etc.), and the witness may believe he sees what he expected to see. If errors of perception are to be attributed to secondary carriers of the viewpoint (witnesses who testify after the fact), they create no stylistic problem. Difficulties arise when the observer carries the primary viewpoint at the time he observes. The possibility of discriminating between his mistaken interpretation and the basic narrative, which cannot be invalid, relies on ambiguity. In the following extract from *The Bowstring Murders,* by Carr Dickson (John Dickson Carr), a candid observer, Tairlaine, carries the point of view:

> Lord Rayle was coming now. The hurrying, quick creak and slap of his shoes drifted to him from the corridor. Up out of it popped the white-robed figure, muttering to itself. Tairlaine sat up. "Ah," he called. "You're here at la—" He might have expected it. Goat-faced growled something into his neck and pounced at the door in the armor hall.

Tairlaine is fooled by an impersonator who wears no makeup. Except for the definite article, "the white-robed figure" is neutral. And it may be alleged that the nickname "goat-faced" need only be taken as a descriptive metaphor on the level of the basic narrative, though it is equivalent to "Lord Rayle" from Tairlaine's standpoint. But were the faces of the impersonator and Lord Rayle so similar that they could constitute a factor of mistaken identification?

The use of the name itself, "Lord Rayle," can be justified by the difference between hearing and sight. The phrase "was coming now" and the sentence that follows sufficiently show that the identification is based only on auditory evidence. "Goat-faced" might be justified in the same way. It would not refer to visual evidence but to an inference from auditory evidence. Tairlaine would have associated the facial traits of Lord Rayle with his way of speaking: "He might have expected it." So the passage would both indicate and conceal the following sequence: Tairlaine makes a definite identification on the basis on auditory evidence (footsteps). The identification is confirmed by visual evidence (white-robed figure) and further auditory evidence (muttering, growling), which trigger an imaginative assumption: "Goat-faced." The text has intimated that, in this particular scene, the visual evidence was of poor quality; the white-robed figure does not come close to Tairlaine.

Despite these precautions, the author seems to have felt that he had better forestall a possible objection: is this passage sufficiently different from others so that it can be interpreted as ambiguous while other passages cannot? One of Tairlaine's statements, "Nobody has come out that door at any time," is buttressed by this free comment: "And, as later events proved, Tairlaine spoke the absolute truth." At another point a footnote is added: "Let it be noted that these statements are true in every particular." These extraneous comments help a wary reader to focus his suspicions on the quoted passage. An unwary reader, on the other hand, might assume that they provide the reliability of Tairlaine's viewpoint with a blanket guarantee. This is fine. At the same time, it must be acknowledged that these comments detract from the integrity of the narrative as such.

In *And Then There Were None,* ten people are isolated on a small island. It soon becomes obvious that one of them has lured the others to this secluded spot in order to kill them one by one. The narrative proceeds from one death to the next, ten in all. The character who apparently dies last, by her own hand, must not be the murderer. The presentation of one of the other deaths must involve a trick. One of the characters is a doctor who establishes the death of Justice Wargrave. The judge, who is the murderer, has enlisted his help on the pretext of thwarting the murderer's plan. The doctor's statement is supposedly enough to make the other characters misinterpret what they see. When everybody else has been disposed of, the judge kills himself. This is revealed in a confession that the judge has enclosed in a bottle thrown into the sea. The bottle is retrieved so as to provide a denouement.

The choice of Wargrave as the murderer is well-justified. The murders look like sentences delivered by a judge: at one point the characters listen to a recording of Wargrave, who accuses them. And the first of the viewpoints adopted by the narrative is that of Wargrave, that is to say, of the planner.

The viewpoint jumps from one character to another. All of them are suspects, one is the murderer, and the story projects their thoughts with apparently the same degree of openness. *And Then There Were None* offers a brilliant example of this technique, though perhaps not a perfect one. To justify some of the passages that constitute Wargrave's thoughts, one may assume that he is trying to adopt the point of view of the others so as to ascertain the soundness of his plan in his own mind and rehearse his role as an intended victim. But since he is not presented as an acute schizophrenic, the severance of these truncated thoughts from their accompaniment and background is hard to accept.

The Red Right Hand combines several of the possibilities mentioned above. The whole text adopts the viewpoint of a first-person character. In a way, he is a narrator. But he is not writing after the denouement, nor is he a diarist; he is jotting down notes about what occurred during the preceding hours in order to find out the identity of a murderer who is still at large in the vicinity. In fact, the text cannot be assumed to correspond to these notes. Some passages refer to the present situation, and in the last pages, when the character is attacked, he is no longer writing. So what the text projects is an unbroken inner monologue rather than a written report. It is also to be noted that the evocations of the past do not follow the sequence of events. The reader has to construct this sequence on the basis of interlocking and partially repetitive flashbacks bearing on what the character saw or learned.

To some extent, the monologue is like the rumination of an armchair detective who has to make narrative sense out of the various pieces of information or misinformation at his disposal. But the monologuist's attitude is not that of a detached reasoner. He has become involved by accident, and he has the impression that he is threatened by the murderer and also perhaps by the official investigators, who may doubt his testimony. Indeed, what he remembers is so odd that he himself openly wonders whether he has not suffered a temporary blanking out of consciousness. Besides, the weird coincidences and echoes that accumulate in his monologue and the disjointed manner in which events are evoked allow the reader to wonder whether the narrator is not hiding something of central import, either unconsciously (there is an allusion to divided personalities) or consciously (he would be trying to throw the official investigators off the scent). The name of the monologuist is, appropriately, "Riddle," too appropriately perhaps unless we go along with the parodic aspect of the text.

Legend

TEXTS LABELED "NOVELS" often include fairly precise and abundant geographical and historical details to which the narrated events are tied. Are these pegs designed to perpetrate a hoax, to let the reader interpret the narrative as history rather than fiction? Apparently not, since the books are generally published as "novels" and may even be prefaced with a warning: "All the characters in this book are fictitious." Is it not absurd to state that the characters are fictional and then to let them roam the streets of a real city at a certain historical time?

The purpose seems to be not to make fiction pass for history but to blur the distinction between the two. The text would be designed to be read as legend. If the geographical and historical pegs allude to places, institutions, individuals, and events to which the reader feels he is linked, the seduction of this "realistic" device does not lie in granting more reality to the characters but in suffusing the reader's world with unreality. Transmuted into material for legends, this world would be freed of cognitive uncertainty, practical vicissitudes, and moral concerns.

Seldom have mystery story writers set the plot in a distant past. Agatha Christie's *Death Comes as the End,* which takes place in pharaonic Egypt, is the most notable exception. Spatial distancing also is not common; stories originally intended for an American, British, or French audience most often take place in the United States, Britain, or France, respectively. When the location is a big city, toponymy and topography are respected; changes are made in, for instance, the name of a hotel. Villages are often invented, but their geographical location is roughly indicated. On the whole, mystery stories set their events like ordinary novels, not like fairy tales ("once upon a time"). But, in accord with their peculiarities, they can give a special flavor to the legendary effect, for they are interested in various kinds of disguises, and the function of geographical and historical details in novels may be interpreted as part of a disguise.

In *Le Mystère de la Chambre Jaune,* by Gaston Leroux, the narrator, Sainclair, insists on the factuality of his extraordinary tale: "I do not claim to be an author. 'Author' suggests 'novelist'; and, thank God, the 'mystery of the yellow room' is full enough of tragic horror to do without literature. I am only, and want only to be, a faithful reporter." The same kind of rhetoric can be found in the sequel, *Le Parfum de la Dame en Noir:* "The consequences which this publication is likely to have are too serious for me not to confine myself to an austere, dry, and methodical narrative. I refer those who might believe that this is a detective novel—the abominable word has been uttered—to the Versailles trial. . . . We have only to open the *Gazette des Tribunaux* and leaf through the pages of the leading newspapers. . . ." The heavy irony is accented by the fact that the name of the narrator (Sainclair) differs from that of the author (Gaston Leroux) and that in the second story Rouletabille, the detective, meets a newspaperman named "Gaston Leroux," who is pictured in rather unflattering terms. One might even say that the irony extends to the style, which in both stories is melodramatic rather than austere and dry.

Rouletabille's opponent, Larsan, is so adept at disguises that at one point the narrator wonders with a shudder whether he himself might not be Larsan. Rouletabille will demonstrate that Sainclair is not Larsan and was never possessed by this devil. But what about the relation between the historical author Leroux, the narrator Sainclair, and the fictional character named "Gaston Leroux"? Are they one and the same? If so, the same what? A similar joke occurs in *Les Mémoires de Maigret,* by Simenon. In this particular book, Maigret is allowed to speak for himself and score "inaccuracies" in the way his historiographer, Simenon, has depicted him in other stories.

British and American authors of mystery stories seem to have resorted more often to pen names than have "serious" novelists. In some cases, the adoption of one or more pseudonyms might be regarded as a meek acceptance of a cultural prejudice bearing on detective stories. But one might also wonder whether the peculiarities of the genre did not encourage the author to disguise himself. Of course, a pen name does not dispel the ambiguity; the individual who writes, erases, reads proofs, and receives royalties is not a fictional individual. But it helps one to raise the question, "What's in a name?" or more precisely, "What does a personifying name stand for?" This question preoccupied Kierkegaard, who let his writing personae, each equipped with a name or nickname, reflect upon one another.

Leblanc's Lupin stories push geographical borrowings quite far, particularly regarding the topography and toponymy of Normandy. In *La Comtesse de Cagliostro,* Lupin determines the location of a treasure buried by medieval monks by observing that a Latin sentence alludes to a minor star in the Big Dipper and that the seven major abbeys in Normandy compose the same figure as the most visible stars in this constellation. In *L'Aiguille Creuse,* the "hollow needle" is a well-known rock off the cliffs at Etretat. With Leblanc, Normandy becomes a legendary land, more so perhaps than with Flaubert or Maupassant. But with him, the legendary effect that derives from the mixture of fiction and geography is tinged with irony. There is a vast difference between Emma Bovary hiding an amorous adventure in Rouen and Lupin hiding his booty in the conical rock off Etretat or locating a treasure at Mesnil-sous-Jumièges. The theme of the mask contaminates the relation between geographical and fictional elements. Mesnil-sous-Jumièges and Etretat clearly appear as geographical camouflage for fictional hiding places. Similar remarks could be made about the "historical" lecture of Gutman in *The Maltese Falcon* and the role of the Marquise de Brinvilliers in *The Burning Court.*

Like Leblanc, Simenon uses geographical references with precision. But he avoids what might counteract this realistic device. It is consequently embarrassing to see Maigret, in *Maigret et le Corps sans Tête,* make inquiries about trains leaving for Poitiers from Montparnasse; in reality, trains bound for this destination depart from Paris-Austerlitz, not Paris-Montparnasse. It is as if Sherlock Holmes mistook Paddington for Waterloo. No doubt, Simenon does not depend as much as Freeman Wills Crofts on railroad timetables and networks. Still, he lets the reader take it for granted that the topography and toponymy of Paris are to be carried intact into his novels, at least as far as streets and public buildings are concerned. A reader of mystery stories will judge such oversights with more severity than will a reader of straight novels, for this kind of lapse should occur as a suspicious error in a testimony or as a piece of trickery on the part of the detective. This is not the case in *Maigret et le Corps sans Tête.*

Quite a few authors of detective stories have used the same detective in different books. This policy is more reminiscent of epic cycles than of novels where some characters reappear (as in Balzac or Galsworthy). The device provides the reader with reliable axioms. Holmes may disregard the law, but he will not turn out to be the murderer. And the reader will learn to look for certain kinds of clues in the ambiguous declarations of Poirot or Doctor Fell. The device also contributes to a legendary effect. The existence of the character seems to stretch beyond the discontinuous adventures that are narrated. This makes him similar to historical individuals about whom we can have only partial information. But in the case of a historical individual, pieces of evidence are of various kinds.

What the reappearance of a detective makes acutely questionable is the use of the word "individual" for fictional as well as historical entities. It is advisable to keep the term for characters within one self-contained mystery story, since mystery stories deal with questions of individuation. But it would be better to use the term "figure" for characters who belong to different tales and yet whom we somehow consider as one entity. It is to be noted that, as legendary figure, a character can appear in stories written by independent authors. Thus Boileau and Narcejac have recently borrowed the figure of Arsène Lupin and added two adventures to those written by Leblanc: *Le Secret d'Eunerville* and *La Poudrière*. They are pastiches, if you like, but Leblanc writing a new Lupin or Chandler writing a new Marlowe may also be considered as doing pastiches of Leblanc or Chandler.

Critics contribute to turning a fictional character into a legendary figure. On the one hand they take the character to be fictional, but on the other the vocabulary and syntax of comments and analyses are the same as those applied to historical individuals. In the case of characters with the same name and the same traits appearing in several stories by one author, it is the critic more than the author who has to fuse these characters into one entity. If, for instance, he is dealing with Sherlock Holmes, a critic may be bothered by discrepancies in the way a biographer is bothered by conflicting reports concerning a historical individual. But the critic will not have the advantage of being able to look outside for decisive documents.

In the domain of "serious" literature, scholars have been busy transmuting "great" authors rather than their characters into legendary figures and cultural idols. They have treated authors as beings who can indistinctly consort with historical individuals and fictional characters. Hamlet is a minor legendary star compared to Shakespeare. But Doyle, on the other hand, has been overshadowed by Sherlock Holmes.

Though it can easily become tedious, I prefer the mock-seriousness of Holmesian scholarship to the religiosity of Shakespearian scholarship. With the former, I remain playfully aware that the scholarly detectives are dealing with a fictional character. Holmesian scholarship may even be regarded as a parody of Shakespearian scholarship. Rex Stout has demonstrated, with an ingenuity worthy of Holmes, that Watson was a woman. I shall applaud the scholar who will demonstrate that "Shakespeare" and "Marlowe" are pen names of Queen Elizabeth and, in an appendix, that he, the scholar, is a reincarnation of Joan of Arc.

Atmosphere

QUITE A FEW MYSTERY STORIES emphasize the closure of the fictional field by concentrating the investigative sequence as well as the investigated events in a narrow space: a secluded house, a train, a ship, a small island, a village. If the riddle has to do with a hermetically sealed room, a potent image of the closure of the field is offered within the fiction.

The esthetic treatment of place is the main element in the creation of an atmosphere. Some mystery stories, as do some straight novels, proceed very much like inflated dramatic scripts. The decor is described by itself, in greater detail than is usual with stage directions since the novelist must also function as set designer. Once the decor is established, the text sets about projecting what the characters do, but quotations of what characters say often take precedence over descriptions of what they do. I prefer a treatment that integrates space and time, subject and object, human and nonhuman elements. This means that descriptions of settings will be dispersed and will indicate what is perceived at a certain moment by the character who carries the viewpoint. I also prefer texts that avoid summarizing the atmosphere of a place with adjectives like "dismal," "cheerful," "dreary," "menacing," or "wonderful," even when they indicate the impression it makes upon a character. What matters esthetically is the impression conveyed to the reader, not to a character, let alone a nonexistent observer. I find that such imperious adjectives as those above interfere with my appreciation of the atmosphere instead of guiding it. It is the business of a critic, if he insists upon it, to characterize the atmosphere that is created. The business of the storyteller is to create it or provide its elements through selective description. In any case, if it is esthetically worthy, the atmosphere of a fictional space will not be reducible to a few adjectives.

The integration of time and space, subject and object, human and nonhuman elements is a narrative application of the Symbolist or Impressionist motto: "A landscape is a mood." This motto would become relevant to mystery stories in particular if it could be made to yield: "A landscape is a clue." The poetic mystery of the landscape would thus be partially turned into a secret to be disclosed. Some hermeneutic tales illustrate this tendency.

Simenon's stories emphasize spatial intimacy. Maigret is not simply an observer; he soaks up the atmosphere, digests it as it were. Notations relating to smell and taste play a part, and the latter extends beyond what Maigret smokes, eats, and drinks. He is not content to put himself imaginatively in the place of other characters in order to surmise their motivations, their reactions to each other. Their social milieu and their dramatic inter-relations are not abstracted from the pervasive material-ity of their existence. Maigret is not satisfied with a dra-matic sketch; he is after a comprehensive feel. His empathy goes deeper than sympathy or antipathy. This allows him to appear quite involved, and yet to bring about the downfall of a murderer without hesitation or grave concern even if he feels some sympathy toward him. In his own way, Maigret remains—like his ratiocinat-ing or adventurous colleagues—an esthete.

He turns to advantage dry bits of information, ob-tained directly or through police facilities. But the im-pression produced by the most characteristic Maigret stories is that the denouement does not result from as-tute inferences. It rather derives, on the one hand, from this global feel that somehow supplies Maigret's con-sciousness with the missing part and, on the other, from the physical presence of Maigret, which, planting itself insistently in the world of suspects and murderer, acts as a catalyst. This is especially noticeable in *Pietr le Letton* or *La Tête d'un Homme,* both of which leave hardly any doubt about the identity of the murderer.

Maigret's method, or lack of method, has been lik-ened to Bergsonian intuition. But two qualifications should be made. Bergson oddly divorces time from space; with Simenon or Maigret, on the other hand, there is no "lived time" without "lived space." Further-more, Bergson considers his type of intuition to be a means of philosophical understanding, not a means to determine events or physical facts; this is left to science.

As fictional detective, Maigret is empowered to extract what happened from atmospheric understanding. A real Maigret, of course, would be at least as fallible as a real Dupin.

Some mystery stories use odd conjunctions and appearances of impossibility to produce a surrealistic kind of atmosphere. In *Le Roman policier français de 1900 à 1970,* Jean-Jacques Tourteau notes that poetry can "steal its way through the rift between mystery and logic" and bathe decors and characters in a "surreal light."

Surrealistic evocations may be content with unusual encounters. Speaking of Pierre Véry's mystery stories in his *Mythologie du roman policier,* Francis Lacassin recalls the juxtaposition of an umbrella and a sewing machine on a dissecting table, an example that André Breton had drawn from Lautréamont; normally these objects are not found in spatial proximity. Surrealistic evocations may also be definitely fantastic, may present us with impossible conjunctions, or may break some rule of individuation. For instance, Breton's "revolver with white hair" is a monstrous individual if it is construed as hair growing on, not simply glued to, a revolver.

In his "Defence of Detective Stories," published at the beginning of the twentieth century, Chesterton says that such stories are "the earliest and only form of popular literature in which is expressed some sense of the poetry of modern life." And he associates modern life with big cities: "The lights of the city begin to glow like innumerable goblin eyes, since they are the guardians of some secret, however crude, which the writer knows and the reader does not. Every twist of the road is like a finger pointing to it; every fantastic skyline of chimney-pots seems wildly and derisively signalling the meaning of the mystery." Two decades later, Aragon in *Le Paysan de Paris* and Breton in *Nadja* will endeavor to turn Paris into a treasure chest of surrealistic "marvels."

Yet Chesterton's Father Brown does not always operate in London. In *The Honour of Israel Gow*, he finds a surrealistic collection of clues in a Scottish castle, a "Gothic" setting. Surrealistic effects do not rely so much on big cities as on manufactured objects. If there is any poetry at all in the evocation of an umbrella and a sewing machine on a dissecting table, it is because it denies the practical function that seems essential to these objects. Bric-à-brac shops and flea markets are ready-made surrealistic settings. Monsters such as the revolver with white hair are created through a fanciful hybridization of machine and animal.

John Dickson Carr is one of the mystery story writers most partial to surrealistic and Gothic effects. In *To Wake the Dead* he lets Doctor Fell express some thoughts about fantastic events: "To the quietest human being seated in the quietest house, there will sometimes come a wish for the possibilities or impossibilities of things. He will wonder whether the tea-pot may not suddenly begin to pour out honey or sea-water; the clock point to all hours of the day at once; the door open upon a lake or a potato-field instead of a London street. Humph, ha. So far, so good. For a reverie or a pantomime it is all very well. But, regarded as a scheme of everyday life, it is enough to make a man shiver."

What should rather be said is that, by themselves,

exceptions to patterns of individuation cannot constitute a "scheme." If a narrative is not to veer into a prose poem, the intervention of fantastic events has to be restricted, especially in a hermeneutic story, where they are to be explained away. And, if an atmosphere is to be created through surrealistic rather than Symbolist means, fantastic events or weird encounters had better be concentrated in a few potent elements. Otherwise, they tend to cancel one another. The creation of an atmosphere is not one of the assets of *Alice in Wonderland.* Mystery stories generally confine surrealistic elements to the border between investigative sequence and investigated events.

Like Breton in *Nadja,* or Boris Vian in *L'Ecume des Jours,* mystery story writers avoid explanations dependent on some supernatural code. Father Brown acknowledges only the miracles that can be attributed to his god, and he takes such care not to come across any of them that his investigations sometimes look like crusades against gods he believes to be false. But an orthodox Surrealist would refrain from any kind of explanation; what is odd or fantastic would remain so. In *Nadja,* Breton characterizes as "signals" the uncanny occurrences that fascinate him. Adopting the perspective of an esthete, he wonders whether a human life is not like a "cryptogram." But he does not attempt to crack the code. And his question, "Who am I?" does not even make clear what kind of answer he is seeking. It is also to be noted that, while he is content to attribute the sibylline signals to "objective chance," surrealistic clues are most often, though not always, the results of someone's activities in detective stories. In *To Wake the Dead,* Doctor Fell lays down the following principle: "Outside things must not act on the criminal; he must act on them."

In *The Honour of Israel Gow,* Inspector Craven is baffled by what he found in Glengyle Castle: "By no stretch of fancy can the human mind connect snuff and diamonds and wax and loose clockwork." Father Brown disagrees. Before giving the "true" explanation, he sketches three fanciful theories that might be used by mystery story writers. And he adds: "Ten false philosophies will fit the universe; ten false theories will fit Glengyle Castle. But we want the real explanation of the castle and the universe." The analogy is acceptable but only on the ground that, like the solution decreed by a fictional detective, a philosophical cosmology can be neither true nor false. In order to claim that a philosophy provides the "true" explanation of the universe, must we not act as if, like Father Brown, we were fictional characters in a fictional universe?

The surrealistic collection of objects found in the castle is the result of Israel Gow's activities, but it was not his intention to puzzle anyone. In *The Chinese Orange Mystery,* by Ellery Queen, on the other hand, the bizarre appearance of the victim and of the scene of the crime is intended by the murderer. He turned everything backwards, in particular the victim's clothes, "in order to conceal the fact that he was a priest, to conceal the fact that his victim wore no necktie and wore a turned-round collar." Supposedly, if the murderer had been content to turn the collar around, "it would have stood out like a sore thumb" because of the absence of a necktie. Actually, in *The Chinese Orange Mystery* as well as in *The Honour of Israel Gow,* the baffling effect is mostly due to stylistic artifice.

Destiny

DESTINY IS THE esthetic cogency of a process. To produce an impression of destiny, the components of the process must appear as means to an end: the denouement achieves the goal. In this perspective, obstacles are means; they prevent the goal from being achieved at once, they allow the cogency to be that of a process. The goal may coincide to some extent with the aims of one or several of the personified individuals involved. But it should transcend them all; destiny is an impersonal finality.

In everyday life, we sometimes have the feeling that certain events are linked to others in a way that goes beyond explanations by causal laws or practical planning. The events seem to be plotting or seem to have been conspiring together. Biographers are tempted to extend this impression to a human life, conveniently simplified, organized, and stylized. A writer of fiction can apply himself to the task with more honesty. And the reader of fiction will not feel like setting up some personified divine planner to explain the impression of a conspiracy between the invented events. If the feeling of freedom is the experience of being one with what signifies (which is what determines), the esthetic enjoyment of a narrative shows how freedom and destiny are to be allied: the coherence of what narrates (plane of freedom) is reflected in what is narrated (plane of destiny).

It is when a story is read for the second time, when an acquaintance with the whole bears on each episode, that the narrated events can most clearly manifest an appearance of destiny. And of course it is then also that some elements can most clearly appear superfluous or poorly connected with the rest of the process. But if the reader approaches a text with the assumption that he is dealing with a mystery story, he is already provided with a rough idea of the goal and result of the process on first reading. Furthermore, a mystery story stresses the interplay between investigated events and investigative sequence so that, to some extent, they determine each other. The final crystallization postdetermines the events that gave rise to the investigative process. A reader of mystery stories is attentive to the dual direction of the signals. More insistently yet more secretively than in a straight narrative, events in a mystery tale point forward and backward.

My outlook on narratives differs from that of plot analysts in the tradition of Vladimir Propp, who derived his method from an examination of folk tales. The objective of this school is to reduce various characters, situations, or episodes to a few functional terms whose arrangement is open to a few variations. Their scientific ambition is opposed to esthetic judgments. However "subjective" my tastes may be, I, on the contrary, do not try to divorce narrative nature from narrative value. Following are a few remarks regarding an application of functional analysis to hermeneutic stories.[4]

Like folk tales, mystery stories stress the functions of characters. But before the denouement is reached, they stress them interrogatively. One might think of applying the following pattern to classical detective stories: the hero is summoned; he undergoes tests whose nature, number, and order would have to be determined; he basks in his triumph. This pattern is suggested and derided in a passage of *Das Versprechen,* by Friedrich Duerrenmatt: "You build your plots logically, like a chess game; here the criminal, here the victim, here the accomplice, here the mastermind. The detective needs only to know the rules and play the game, and he has the criminal trapped, has won a victory for justice." Actually, detective stories often take care to distinguish the detective's success from a victory of legal justice. Besides, while the plot may appear to the reader to be constructed as Duerrenmatt's character intimates once the story has been read, this is not the way it develops and is to be appreciated when it is read for the first time. "Here the criminal . . . here the accomplice." Where? "Here the victim." But the identity of the victim may be in doubt, or there may be no victim at all. "Here the mastermind (detective)." Possibly, but if the perspective is not confined to classical detective stories, the detective may turn out to be the murderer; he may fail, or there may be no detective at all. To do justice to hermeneutic stories, plot diagrams would have to take into account the interrogative aspect of the functions.

They would also have to pay some attention to the

viewpoint. This factor, perhaps secondary in folk tales, is essential in mystery stories. The examples given in the section on viewpoint show how it complicates matters. And they also show that carrying the primary viewpoint is a function that cannot be placed on the same level as others.

In *The Poisoned Chocolates Case* a table compares several aspects of the solutions offered by several investigators. In *The Three Coffins* Doctor Fell takes time out to sketch a classification of locked-room puzzles. This table and this sketch are not concerned with the ways investigative sequences develop; yet they have something to do with plots, the plots that are concealed. Formal analyses of hermeneutic tales should classify investigated plots as well as investigative plots. They may be difficult to separate; quite a few mystery stories develop the two plots concomitantly instead of stating the problem at the start.

In *The Scarlet Letters,* by Ellery Queen, the murder occurs near the end. But the reader does not simply have to wonder whether there will be a murder and, if so, who will kill whom; the way the murder happens is a clue to what was concealed in the narration of the preceding events. In *The Spy Who Came In from the Cold,* Leamas, a British agent, believes he is taking part in a plot to ruin Mundt, a chief of East German intelligence, by persuading the East Germans that he is a traitor. Mundt manages to turn the tables on his accusers. Leamas then realizes that the full scope of the British plan has been hidden from him, as it has been from the reader, since Leamas carries the viewpoint. Mundt is indeed working with the

British and the objective of the operation was to help him get rid of a dangerous competitor in East German intelligence.

In such texts as *The Maltese Falcon,* or Chandler's *Farewell, My Lovely,* private detectives have to expose their employers. Leamas differs from them; while he performs his role as a tricked trickster, he does not investigate anything. Yet the development is an investigative sequence from the standpoint of a reader who suspects that something is concealed from the unsuspecting Leamas. Like Spade or Marlowe, Leamas discovers the "truth." But the story ends with his death. *The Spy Who Came In from the Cold* shows quite clearly that the goal of hermeneutic tales is not a triumph of legal justice and does not even have to include the practical triumph of characters for whom the reader is induced to feel some sympathy. It also shows how inadequate and misleading formal diagrams based on categories derived from the analysis of folk tales would be if they were applied to mystery stories.

And yet hermeneutic tales do offer remarkable resemblances to each other. Can similarities in plots contribute to an impression of destiny? A reader who has become accustomed to the habits of a writer or a school will recognize patterns of events in narratives that exemplify these habits. But if destiny is an esthetic order that differs from causal routine, it must also be distinguished from esthetic routine. A sense of destiny can emanate from narrated events to the extent that they appear to compose their own spatiotemporal scheme instead of simply illustrating causal laws or esthetic conventions, in other words, to the extent that they signal one another under their particular aspect rather than under some general aspect. Destiny is sensed despite and beyond generality. But while uniqueness is directly apprehended by sensibility, the intellect can only project the particular as an ideal limit of the generic and actuality as an ideal limit of possibility. If I try to account for the impression of destiny that a narrated process made upon me, I shall have to bring out connections of a more or less general type. In this respect, an analysis of destiny is bound to be as unsatisfactory as an analysis of atmosphere. By definition destiny, which is to time what atmosphere is to space, must remain somewhat inexplicable. An analysis can point toward the echoes that are sensed between the events, but it cannot register them. And, of course, these echoes may be experienced as insignificant rather than potent, dissonant rather than consonant by another reader according to his temperament, background, and even his mood.

In *A Study in Scarlet* and in *The Sign of the Four,* Holmes sums up his gifts as an ability to reason backward, to infer events from traces. But the determination of causes also involves some reasoning forward: effect A may be caused by an event of type X or Y; events of type X, but not of type Y, leave trace B; so look for B. Besides, as he takes into account the intentions of other characters, the detective cannot be content with causal reasoning. In *The Sign of the Four,* Holmes has to determine where his opponent has decided to hide. One might try to reduce his thinking to reasoning from cause to effect: the assumed intention of the opponent would be the anterior event and his move the subsequent event. But this will not do, for an intention is not an event. A decision may be presented as an event, but the purpose or goal is what makes the events into means. The purpose unites the process, allows its components to be detached from other events. The detective's causal reasoning rests on a finalistic tie. It is also to be noted that, when he trusts a client's report or his own memory, a detective like Holmes does not interpret indicators of past events in a causal way. In theory, they may be considered as effects—memory traces, etc.—but the detective exploits them as linguistic or imaginative (iconic) signs, not as causal signals.

In classical detective-and-opponent stories, the investigated events are primarily tied by the opponent's purpose and the investigative events by the detective's purpose. The former is subordinated to the latter: what is concealed is to be absorbed by what is not. As loser, the detective's antagonist is his accomplice; the conflict resolves into a conspiracy. If the detective's opponent stops acting before the intervention of the detective, the latter's investigation can develop into a sequence of events if he has to look for clues other than those he has been initially given or if he has to prove his theory by producing a decisive clue, by recovering a stolen document, for example, or implementing a scheme to catch his opponent. If the opponent remains active, investigated events and investigative sequence are concomitant and thus tied more closely from a narrative standpoint.

But from the reader's standpoint, esthetics demand that the timing and content of the denouement look appropriate. This perspective differs from that of the fictional detective, even if he is pictured as an esthete. It would be misleading for the reader to try to emulate the detective's thinking process; the mastermind is a red herring. Some detectives claim that their solution is causally necessary and that absolute certainty could not be attained earlier. This is at best a claim of esthetic congruence. Actually, why it takes so long for the mastermind to mate his opponent is often a bothersome question. To save his reputation, the detective sometimes announces that he has deciphered the enigma and then, on some pretext, postpones the revelation, even though the delay results in further unpleasantness; apparently his reasoning forward is not on a par with his reasoning backward. As for Hercule Poirot, he has been known to confess not of course that he is but at least that he was "an imbecile."

The investigative sequence should result not only in a figuration of what is concealed but also in its own transfiguration. Striking denouements have been obtained by a conjunction of apparently incompatible functions: murderer and victim, murderer and detective, murderer and ally of the detective. The choice of a primary carrier of the viewpoint as murderer is in a special class, since the function of narrator or primary observer is not on the same level as others. The content, if not the timing, of the denouement will be esthetically appropriate if it exploits a pattern emphasized in the quest and if it manages deeply to alter the global picture through a simple modification. This strategy is comparable to changing a 6 into a 9, the sum of two threes into their product. Agatha Christie's denouements are often good in this respect.

In *Five Little Pigs,* Poirot investigates the murder of a man who is believed to have been killed by his wife because he was going to leave her. Poirot decides that his mistress killed the man instead, for the same reason. In *Dead Man's Folly,* Poirot declares: "I think, *mon ami,* that Lady Stubbs is dead. And I will tell you why I think that. It is because Mrs. Folliat thinks she is dead." This will be confirmed in the denouement. But when these words are uttered, they seem to allude to the present Lady Stubbs, who is really an impostor substituted for the murdered woman. Poirot is right in assuming that Mrs. Folliat thinks Lady Stubbs is dead; she knows. But he does not interpret his own words in this way. His statement is an example of dramatic irony.

In *Peril at End House* it seems that attempts are made on a girl's life because of an inheritance and that her cousin was killed because the cousin was mistaken for her. The transfiguration consists in decreeing that the threatened girl faked the attempts on her own life and killed her cousin. The motive remains the same, and the ending shows that she was indeed threatened, but by Poirot, who had acted as her protector during one of his spells of imbecility.

The inversion is even simpler in *Thirteen at Dinner (Lord Edgware Dies).* A woman is believed to have been in a certain place while an impersonator was in another place. All that has to be done is to switch locations. Here again Poirot acts as if he had never read an Agatha Christie. In *Murder at the Vicarage,* two characters confess separately, apparently because they are in love and want to protect each other. It will finally be decided that they were indeed in love and wanted to protect each other, but they also attempted to protect themselves by means of easily refuted confessions. They were in it together. This is a Hegelian strategy: thesis and antithesis are superseded by a synthesis. But the other suspects are left out of the equation. For a more comprehensive application, one should turn to *Murder in the Calais Coach (Murder on the Orient Express).* The twelve suspects give one another an alibi. Solution: a conspiracy. They acted as self-appointed jurors and executioners. *L'Assassin habite au 21,* by Steeman, provides a similar example.

So far, I have dwelt on the content of the denouement, on the relation between mask and face. What about the order of events in the investigative sequence? A parade of witnesses, a methodical or haphazard accumulation of evidence cannot by themselves convey an impression of esthetically ordered events. The moves of active antagonists can be related according to a stimulus-and-response dialectic: a detective seeks a witness; the hidden opponent kills the witness before he can be reached; this move provides a clue that incites the detective to look for a piece of corroborative evidence; the opponent destroys it. But this dialectic, by itself, constitutes a practically rather than esthetically cogent sequence of events.

Some mystery stories try to make the narrated sequence echo an emblematic pattern. *And on the Eighth Day,* by Ellery Queen, is permeated with a biblical atmosphere. The detective, Ellery Queen, stumbles upon a small religious community that has remained isolated in a western desert for a hundred years. He is taken to be "Elroy Quenan," who, according to oral tradition, is to be sent to the community in time of trouble to discover the truth. Subsequent events are also linked to prophecy or to biblical incidents. Wisely, I think, the text pokes fun at its own portentousness. The sacred book of the community, the book of "Mk'h," had been lost, but it was thought to be recovered at the store which is the only link between the community and the rest of the world. It is in a language unknown to the members of the community, but they have been impressed by the initials on the cover. The book is indeed of the prophetic kind; it is Hitler's *Mein Kampf.*

In the 1930s, it was a fashion among French dramatists to write variants of well-known classical tragedies. British and American mystery story writers, on the other hand, preferred nursery rhymes. Like hermeneutic tales, nursery rhymes are partial to weird occurrences. A nursery rhyme may be used to yield a clue to the solution. There is also the possibility of a parallel between the investigative episodes of a mystery tale and the items in a nursery rhyme; analogies between the parts and identical order will produce a homology between the two series. Taken by itself, each series may be poorly connected. But if there is a homology, the investigative process will appear to obey a pattern that differs from a general law. Furthermore, while the series of events evoked in a nursery rhyme is causally gratuitous, improbable, or impossible, while it is devoid of practical reason, it is not without rhyme, it is not without poetic reason. A nursery rhyme can thus superimpose an esthetic consistency on an investigative sequence that otherwise could claim only practical links. The difficulty lies in integrating the emblematic pattern in such a way that it does not merely look elaborately ornamental, like a series of epigraphs at the heads of chapters.

In *The Rasp*, by Philip MacDonald, the name of the victim, "Hoode," suggests "Who killed Cock Robin?" to the detective. But this is only a passing allusion with no emblematic value. In *Five Little Pigs*, the pig motif is used more elaborately but just as superficially as in *The Rasp*. It serves only to characterize the suspects. It has nothing to do with the sequence of events, except for the fact that Poirot has to interview one "little pig" after another. In *There Was an Old Woman*, by Ellery Queen, the nursery rhyme that furnishes the titles of the book and of some chapters is used in a similar fashion: it depicts the suspects in the detective's eyes. Allusions to other folkloric motifs also crop up in the tale. The theme is used mostly as an atmospheric element. Functionally, it yields only a deceptive clue: it seems to point to a suspect who is writing "a modern Mother Goose." In *The Bishop Murder Case*, by Van Dine, a series of murders is reminiscent of several nursery rhymes. An ambiguous "bishop" also plays a part: chess piece and character in a play by Ibsen. Here again these allusions do not provide the episodes with a sequential model.

The device is used more impressively in *And Then There Were None*. It is soon made clear that the murderer is going to pattern his series of killings after "Ten Little

Indians." Acting to some extent as the author's mouth-piece, the murderer notes in a confession that is to be stuffed in a bottle and thrown into the sea: "A childish rhyme of my infancy came back into my mind—the rhyme of the ten little Indian boys. It had fascinated me as a child of two—the inexorable diminishment—the sense of inevitability." As soon as it is disclosed to the reader, the emblem functions as an oracle that announces not only that the ten characters will die one by one but also that the manner and order of their deaths, as they are overtly presented, will reflect those of the deaths of the ten little Indians. The emblem also offers clues to the identity of the murderer. The sense of inevitability would appeal to a judge, as one of the characters is allowed to point out: "He's played God Almighty for a good many months every year. That must go to a man's head eventually. He gets to see himself as all-powerful, as holding the power of life and death—and it's possible that his brain might snap and he might want to go one step farther and be Executioner and Judge extraordinary." There is no mur-derer in the jingle, but a judge does not consider himself to be a murderer. Besides, in the version that is used the last little Indian brings the process to a close by hanging himself, which is also what appears to occur in the story. Hanging was the capital sentence that the murderer used to deliver as a British judge. On the other hand, the reader also expects the emblematic pattern to function as a deceptive clue. He expects the character who, ac-cording to the apparent sequence, dies last not to be the answer to the riddle. He expects one of the other deaths to be faked.

The story sets upon itself conditions so exacting that it has to accumulate improbabilities. I do not mean improbabilities from an external standpoint; cognitive standards regarding probability are irrelevant. I mean dissonances between the methodical thoroughness of the murderer's plan and the contingencies on which it relies. To say that the murderer's mind is deranged would be a psychological excuse, not an esthetic justification. These dissonances illustrate the difficulty I mentioned. *And Then There Were None* integrates the emblem by making it part of the murderer's plan. It yields clues and imposes an impressive pattern on the development. But its integration also results in a discrepancy in the nature of the plan. In any case, to convey an impression of destiny the narrated events must appear to conspire in a way that goes beyond the application of what a personified character may plan. Destiny is an impersonal finality or the fictional reflection of the impersonal finality of the narrative.

Dramatic conflicts can be arranged so as to yield an impersonal conspiracy. A tight interaction between the various goals of the characters can result in a denouement that is neither wanted nor foreseen by any character. In tragedies, revelation is allied to downfall. The hero who achieves a tragic recognition brings about his doom. Oedipus succeeds as a detective; he sees the "truth." So he must blind himself and sentence himself to exile. When he understands that he has been "framed" by the oracles, by treacherous linguistic clues, he has to disappear. *Oedipus Rex* suggests an esthetic definition of hybris. A character is out of his place if he arrogates to himself the goal of the total process. If as a hero he is allowed to discover the secret of this goal, this disclosure spells his elimination. But tragedies are wont to hide the application of esthetic justice with a religious mask; the gods or a social imperative "punish" the hybristic individual.

I have noted that detective story writers have tried in various ways to counteract the effect of a triumphant detective. A story like *And Then There Were None* gets rid of the detective but reinforces the role of the mastermind. The murderer dies, but it was part of his plan to kill himself. The development and result of the process conform to his goal.

In *The Spy Who Came In from the Cold*, Leamas, the carrier of the viewpoint, is simply led to understand what happened, and he neither plans nor foresees the way in which he dies. The place where he dies deserves a note. Mystery story writers are often careless about the location of the last episode; the detective delivers the solution from his armchair, or he is content to choose the place where the investigation began. In *The Spy Who Came In from the Cold* Leamas dies on the Berlin Wall, the emblem of the conflict between East and West and also of the conspiracy between Mundt and British intelligence. The story is designed to give an impression of destiny as far as Leamas is concerned. But what is revealed to him and to the reader is a successful human conspiracy. True, the death of Leamas does not seem to have been planned by the conspirators, at least by the British party. But if the text is considered as a hermeneutic story, his death belongs to an epilogue; the revelation of what had been concealed has already taken place.

Some narratives insert events that are not intended by any character to be analogical clues but which in fact have this value. In particular, they serve as catalysts that allow the detective's thinking to crystallize. In *Peril at End House,* by Agatha Christie, a chance remark of the narrator about abbreviations of names points to the possibility that two characters, so far labeled with a nickname and an abbreviation, may have the same official name. In *The Scarlet Letters,* by Ellery Queen, the victim manages to trace "XY" before dying. His message appears to be based on a code that he used to designate places. The detective presumes that he meant to complete the message with a Z. So he goes to the Bronx Zoo, which corresponds to Z in the code. He finds nothing there, but he observes a workman repainting the faded entrance sign: "NEW YORK ZOOLOGICAL——something, it said." The painter starts on the G and stops. At this point the detective is enlightened. The solution is carefully veiled; the assumption that the message was to end with Z (the zoo), the undisclosed "something" in the entrance sign, and the fact that the unfinished letter is a G are "false" scents. The analogical clue is that the unfinished letter G looks like a C: the dying man did not intend to complete XY as XYZ but as XX, indicating that he was double-crossed.

The painter's clue bears on the investigative sequence only globally and retrospectively. *The Gold Bug*, by Poe, exploits a coincidence in a more potent and intricate way. The main character, the one whose "will" the events as they are narrated appear to obey, is not a personified character. It is not Legrand (despite his "greatness") or Jupiter (despite his divine name) or Captain Kidd (though he acts posthumously as a tricky character); it is the individual indicated in the title. The finding of the beetle generates the sequence and points to what is concealed using two types of connections: practical connections (odd at first, then spurious) and analogical connections. Only the odd practical connections play a part in Legrand's investigation. But the story does not follow Legrand's activities. He proceeds from cipher to treasure, whereas the narrative proceeds from treasure to cipher. In this respect, though it includes a ratiocinative and successful detective, *The Gold Bug* is not a classical detective story. It is to be noted that, when the clue is a cipher similar to the one proposed in *The Gold Bug*, the reader who wants to emulate the detective has to sit back and work at the decoding for himself. By rejecting the emergence of the cipher in a sort of epilogue, *The Gold Bug* avoids the possibility of such a break in the enjoyment of the narrative, at least of its essential part. The main objective of this hermeneutic tale, as it is told, is not to reveal the solution of a cipher, but to reveal that there was a cipher.

The beetle is oddly practical, first because of its presence (to avoid being bitten, Jupiter picks up a piece of parchment half-buried in the sand), then because of its absence (Legrand draws it on the parchment). The importance of the parchment is veiled at this stage by its being called "paper" and also by the fact that its proximity to a piece of wreckage is not mentioned. However, there is a vague esthetic clue: Legrand's hobby is to search for "shells or entomological specimens," and the carcass of a boat is a kind of shell. The scarab turns "or" into "and." The word "shell" also foreshadows the skull drawn on the parchment and the skull on the branch.

When the narrator joins Legrand again, the practical role of the beetle becomes a hoax; Legrand tries to mystify the narrator. He says: "I sent for you that I might have your assistance in furthering the views of Fate and of the bug." The conjunction between "Fate" and "bug" is apposite; their distinction is somewhat deceptive. He also says that Jupiter was right in supposing that the insect was made of real gold. The beetle is going to make Legrand's fortune; he will arrive at the gold of which it is the "index." The right interpretation of "index" is not "trace" or "pointer" but "emblem." Legrand ties the dead scarab to a piece of string and as he walks keeps "twirling it to and fro, with the air of a conjuror." He acts as if the beetle were to function like a divining rod, while it is to be used only as a weight. He finally explains his behavior: "I felt somewhat annoyed by your evident suspicions touching my sanity and so resolved to punish you quietly, in my own way, by a little bit of sober mystification."

The analogical connections are based on the color and on the shape of the insect. In the first part of the story, Legrand draws it on the parchment but the narrator sees a skull drawn on the other side of the parchment. This episode foreshadows the association of the beetle itself with the skull on the branch. The narrator looks at the "wrong" side of the parchment, but it will prove to be the side on which the cipher is inscribed. In the second part Jupiter drops the beetle from the wrong socket, an error that delays the discovery of the treasure. This creates a further analogy, but this time it is combined with a contrast. One might even venture to say that, as it is successively dropped from both sockets, the beetle provides the "antennae" that the narrator thought were missing when he looked at the drawing of a skull, expecting to see a beetle.

When, at the beginning of the second part, Jupiter talks about Legrand, his words conceal the latter's activities; but at the same time they contribute to the set of correspondences. The beetle's bite must have deranged his master's mind. Legrand talks of gold in his sleep. He "keeps a syphon wid de figgurs on de slate" (homophony with "cipher"). And the invitation that the narrator receives from Legrand may be likened to the invitation that Legrand receives from the beetle (a cipher). There is also a correspondence between the "mess of human bones" under which the treasure is buried and the remnants of a boat close to which the piece of parchment is found, both half buried in the sand. One of Mallarmé's short prose pieces is entitled *"Le Démon de l'Analogie."* He also composed a sonnet to honor Edgar Allan Poe.

In his "Casual Notes," Chandler wrote: "It often seems to this particular writer that the only reasonably honest and effective method of fooling the reader that remains is to make the reader exercize his mind about the wrong problem, to make him, as it were, solve a mystery (since he is almost sure to solve something) which will land him in a bypath because it is only tangential to the central problem." To some extent, *The Gold Bug* points in this direction. What can a beetle indicate? In a way, this is the wrong problem; it is not the practical question with which Legrand is concerned. But esthetically this is the main question that the narrative is designed to answer.

The role granted to the beetle bears some resemblance to the part played by "Ten Little Indians" in *And Then There Were None*. The insect and the rhyme generate the narrated sequences, provide clues, reinforce and partially conceal practical ties with esthetic bonds. But the role of the beetle is better suited to produce an impression of destiny. The insect itself is present, whereas the little Indians manifest themselves only in effigy. And prior to the expedition at least, the beetle's function is not dictated by a personified character.

Unlike a drama, which can confine itself to interpersonal conflicts, a story should develop connections between personified characters and other elements. It is these elements that as emblems, not as causal signals or practical tools and obstacles, can yield the correspondences on which an impression of destiny depends. In *L'Etranger,* by Albert Camus, Meursault is content to say that if he committed a murder, it was "because of the sun." Unlike Aeschylus's Orestes, who said: "Because of Loxias," Meursault does not personify the sun as a god. He offers what may pass for a causal explanation: he was overcome by the heat. But what matters in the economy of the story is that he discloses an esthetic clue: though the narrated events do not take place in one day, the sequence of the main episodes is patterned after the journey of the sun. The mother's burial occurs in the morning, the murder at noon. During the trial, Meursault is brought back to his cell in the evening. The story ends at night. This order contrasts with an emphasis on practical absurdity.

Taken by themselves, the practical clues that are offered in *The Red Right Hand*, by Joel Townsley Rogers, make it pretty obvious that the character who presents himself as Professor MacComerou is an impostor. But this is only part of the solution. It will be decided that the impostor is the professor's nephew, Dexter, a garageman who also posed as St. Erme, who in turn is believed to have been murdered. In addition, Dexter briefly assumed the part of a hitchhiker who is believed to have killed St. Erme. Regarding this bewildering set of identities, practical clues are slight, and it is not by using Holmesian reasoning that Doctor Harry Riddle, the monologuist and detective *malgré lui*, will manage to work out the equation. Furthermore, the practical clues that concern the impersonation of the professor by his nephew are veiled by a technique that has been analyzed in the section on viewpoint. And they are buried in an avalanche of treacherous yet significant echoes.

Doctor Harry Riddle of New York has been summoned to operate on a patient in Vermont. The patient dies during the operation. The surgeon journeys back in a car that the Vermont housekeeper asked him to deliver to a garage in New York City. On the same day, Elinor has been driving from New York with her fiancé, St. Erme. Supposedly they are going to be married. In Connecticut they pick up a hitchhiker and near sunset stop by a lake (unabashedly nicknamed "Dead Bridegroom's Pond"). Elinor hears but cannot see a deadly fight between St. Erme and the hitchhiker. Believing that after eliminating St. Erme the hitchhiker is after her, she hides in the woods. The pursuer returns to the car and is seen by several people driving crazily along a country road with the apparently dead or unconscious St. Erme by his side. Riddle's car breaks down at the end of the same country road, but nobody passes him by. Looking for help, he stops at the cottage of MacComerou, whose name he recognizes: as a student, Riddle had used a textbook of MacComerou's on homicidal psychology. Riddle borrows a wrench from MacComerou (actually, MacComerou's nephew, Dexter), repairs the car, drives away, finds and picks up Elinor, and drives back to Mac-Comerou's house, where the police have arrived.

Thus by accident the two journeys meet halfway. Riddle has met not only Elinor but also the murderer, who impersonates his own uncle after having posed as St. Erme and changed clothes with the hitchhiker during his ostentatious drive to make it appear that St. Erme was the victim. The two journeys and the characters that make them are also connected at the journeys' ends, when it is disclosed that Elinor lives opposite Riddle, that she works with a relative of Riddle, and that St. Erme had told her that the goal of their trip was the house of Riddle's patient in Vermont.

To these ties may be added correspondences between Riddle and the hitchhiker. Riddle is a doctor; the hitchhiker gave his name as "Doc." They have reddish hair and the same kind of voice. It is believed that the hitchhiker used a knife and stole fifty fifty-dollar bills; Riddle's patient died under his "knife," and the housekeeper gave him fifty fifty-dollar bills. When he was picked up, the hitchhiker held in his hands a kitten that had been run over; after Riddle's patient died, the nurse told the doctor: "You look like a little boy whose pet kitten has been run over." The lobe of the hitchhiker's left ear was missing; Riddle nicked his left ear with a crank. Another link is provided by the hitchhiker's hat: Riddle recognizes it as an old hat of his that he had thrown away.

These echoes are not practical clues: Riddle and the hitchhiker cannot be the same individual. The similarities contribute to the atmosphere. They lead Riddle to doubt his sanity in conjunction with other details: Mac-Comerou's textbook brings to Riddle's mind the Jekyll-Hyde model; a policeman misunderstands his name and believes he belongs to the Ridder family (involved in a local murder case); a dog chases after his car as if he were "Jack the Ripper." Riddle concentrates his rumination on the hitchhiker and fancies the man is going to appear to him as he writes his notes in front of a mirror in which he can see his own reflection. If Riddle is not the same individual as the hitchhiker, is he not at least a kind of duplicate, playing the same kind of role? Actually, neither Riddle nor the hitchhiker have killed anyone. But under the wrong analogy is hidden the right one: the hitchhiker was a victim, and Riddle is a prospective victim.

Riddle has seen a wailing gray cat near Mac-Comerou's cottage. And he has learned that the hitchhiker held a "mangled gray kitten" in his hands. He checks himself; there is no way in which the two cats could be connected. And yet a psychological clue can be extracted from the association. The hitchhiker's pose is that of a Pietà. The murderer, on the other hand, has abandoned the cat of his uncle, and during his drive he has deliberately hit a dog (a St. Bernard, of course). MacComerou's textbook also contains clues: it alludes to the case of his nephew. And while the reference to Doctor Jekyll and Mr. Hyde is misleading it bears some relation to the fact that the murderer assumes several roles.

When Dexter creeps up behind Riddle, he will appear in the mirror. The same thing must have occurred when the impersonator killed his uncle. Somehow, Riddle had the feeling that the professor was guiding his thinking. Before tangling with Dexter, Riddle manages to slip under the blotter a note that names the murderer. He then discovers that MacComerou had hidden a similar note in the same place: "My nephew Adam M. Dexter is coming behind me now to kill me."

The Riddle-Ridder-Ripper play on names may be regarded as an indirect clue to the fact that the murderer has used several names. The equation between "S. Inis St. Erme" and "sinister me" helps Riddle to shift from St. Erme to Dexter: "sinister" and "dexter" are the Latin translations of "left" and "right" (the text has dutifully alluded to Latin). The title "The Red Right Hand" thus contains the name of the murderer. It refers also to a practical clue: the murderer has cut off the right hand of one of his victims so that the corpse might be wrongly identified as that of St. Erme. Moving from the wrong to the right direction involves a translation from left to right, from the left ears of Riddle and the hitchhiker to the missing right hand of the "wrong" St. Erme, from "S. Inis St. Erme," which means "left," to "Dexter," which means "right."

Finally, I should mention the interplay between Riddle the surgeon and Dexter the garageman. Riddle becomes involved because his car breaks down; he borrows a wrench from Dexter and repairs his car. Dexter steals Riddle's surgical instruments to sever the hand of one of his victims. And it is finally revealed that the garage in New York where Riddle was to deliver the car is Dexter's. Unaccountably, Riddle had pocketed the address without looking at it. Superfluously, the housekeeper had even added: "This is the man" (a salute to Edgar Allan Poe?). Riddle's destination was his apartment, opposite the building where Elinor lives. His destination was also the garage operated by the murderer. Somewhat surprisingly, the story does not specify whether the address had been tucked into a right-hand pocket or not.

The Red Right Hand contains the kind of echoes on which an impression of destiny depends. But it also illustrates factors that are not designed to produce this effect. The overabundance of coincidences and correspondences combines with a cascade of impersonations to turn the text into a comprehensive parody. And the sense of a temporal sequence is blurred by a monologue that projects episodes in a disjointed manner. Analogy plays a part in an impression of destiny. But it must not overshadow succession.

Part III /Cryptogram

Clues as words

TO A CONSIDERABLE EXTENT, the data available to fictional detectives are verbal. Holmes is fond of physical traces, but he has to listen to witnesses. The relations between what a witness says and what is hidden are not limited to the simple oppositions provided by precise lies or mistakes. Testimonies may be vague, incomplete, fanciful, multivalent, or ironical. And they are not the only linguistic clues that occur inside the fiction; apparently irrelevant speech, conversations that are cut short or partially overheard, dying words, partially destroyed letters and documents, and coded messages have often been used. In *The Nine-Mile Walk,* by Harry Kemelman, a series of inferences is triggered by one sentence: "A nine-mile walk is no joke, especially in the rain."

In classical detective stories, the detective himself often indulges in adding a few tricky verbal clues of his own. In *The Tragedy of X,* by Barnaby Ross (a pseudonym of the authors of Ellery Queen stories), the detective is chided for having said that Wood, who was only a role played by Stopes, had been killed by Stopes. The detective then justifies himself and the text: "I did not say that Stopes killed Wood. I said he was responsible for removing Wood from the face of the earth, which is literally true." In other texts, the detective, as well as other characters, is interrupted or stops deliberately when he is about to make a straightforward revelation. John Dickson Carr is too fond of this suspensive device.

In any case, whether or not they are linguistic within the fiction, all clues are linguistic from the standpoint of the reader, and they are provided by one text. A real or fictional investigator may be in a position to check a testimony against a physical trace or an independent testimony; the reader can only compare the elements of one text.

Unlike quoted statements, the basic narrative must not include definitely invalid axioms. This rule is the fundamental condition of a coherent narrative, hence of the unity of the fictional world. It is also a condition of the guessing game. But if the narrative adopts the viewpoint of an observer instead of a *post facto* narrator, its basic part simply consists of operators such as "he thought," "he told himself," or "he interpreted what he saw as." What these operators bind has the same status as a quoted statement, hence they may preface invalid axioms. In most narrative sentences these operators remain implicit. In order to limit the possibilities of trickery that are thus afforded, the text should supply stylistic clues that allow an attentive reader to bracket some but not all narrative statements. On the whole, it is esthetically preferable to prevent fictional observers and experiencers from generating definitely invalid axioms.

Other devices such as vagueness, incompleteness, or ambiguity provide a sufficient variety.

Whether they are within quotation marks or not, descriptions of objects in mystery stories illustrate tricks of
language rather than tricks of perception. Such descriptions generally consist of a substantival part that identifies the category and of an adjectival part that adds
some special traits. Perception infers a category from
some sensory phenomena. Description, on the other
hand, appears to decorate essence with accident. No
doubt some unexpressed errors of perception can be
explained by the proposition that we travel in life with a
collection of ready-made genera and species. But even in
such cases, language does not simply express the error;
it masks and confirms it. It is also to be noted that an
inconspicuous use of the definite article is enough to
turn the identification of a category into the recognition
of an individual: "the man," "the knife."

In *To Wake the Dead,* by John Dickson Carr, the murderer, who has procured a policeman's uniform, con-
trives to pass for an attendant in a hotel whose staff wears
a similar uniform. The text has to furnish some adjectival
clues regarding this similarity. A witness says: "Dark
blue; red strips on the cuff; bars or silver buttons; something like that." But he does not say: "Something like a
policeman's uniform." This omission is well justified in
the case of this particular witness: he expected to see a
hotel attendant in this kind of uniform, and the murderer
carried towels. But a punctilious reader might feel that
the same omission lacks justification when, on entering
the hotel apparently for the first time, the primary carrier

of the perspective fails to notice the remarkable similarity; he simply sees a "neat dark blue uniform."

In Ellery Queen's *The Chinese Orange Mystery* the murderer has turned backwards the clothes of the victim and other objects on the scene of the crime "to conceal the fact that his victim was a priest, to conceal the fact that his victim wore no necktie and wore a turned-round collar." In *To Wake the Dead* the description of the uniform goes with a mistaken identification of the species: hotel attendant uniform. In *The Chinese Orange Mystery,* on the other hand, the description avoids a specific label; it jumps from genus (collar) to noncommittal traits and an assumption that trivializes the collar: "His narrow stiff collar similarly was turned about, clamped with a shiny gold collar-button at the nape." It is the description rather than the murderer that may be said to reduce "clerical collar" to "turned-round collar." What is somewhat bothersome in this case is that the fictional mastermind allows himself to be fooled by the staging without the intervention of a linguistic filter.

In *The Honour of Israel Gow*, the text has to conceal the fact that several objects have been shorn of their gold or gilded parts. Two descriptive items provide pretty obvious clues: "Precious stones, without their settings" and "wax candles, without candlesticks." Others are more evasive, and since it is the collection that is emphasized, what is evasive helps to cover what is obvious, as in "Minute pieces of metal, some like steel springs and some in the form of microscopic wheels"; "little Catholic pictures. . . . We only put them in the museum because they seem curiously cut about and defaced." The text projects the responsibility for the deceptive descriptions onto the inspector who enumerates the clues to Father Brown. Does this device constitute a sufficient justification? The inspector identifies the pieces of metal as "clockwork." Why then does he choose to be crafty at first and say "like steel springs," "in the form of microscopic wheels"? Besides, even if the inspector may be assumed to know little about "Catholic pictures," the same cannot be said of Father Brown. How is it that when the latter views the evidence he does not notice at once that what is cut out is the gilded part of the pictures? The insertion of three fanciful theories, put forward by Father Brown before the enumeration is completed, is a more legitimate and quite amusing device. These explanations are at once declared to be wrong, but they help confuse the reader.

Another means of concealment, which is more effective in long stories, is the distancing of related descriptions. What matters in this case is not the temporal distance between fictional events but the distance in reading time, in other words, between printed pages. It is the reader's memory, not that of a character, that is to be tested. In *The White Priory Murders,* by Carter Dickson, a car is described on page 29: "From its massive silvered radiator-cap to the streamlined letters CINEARTS STUDIOS, INC. painted along the side, it was conspicuous enough for the eye of Tim Emery, who drove it." The car is described again on page 121: "Emery's gaudy yellow car, with CINEARTS STUDIO sprawled in shouting letters across it and the thin bronze stork above a smoking radiator." Apart from the distance, three stylistic factors contribute to concealing the change in radiator-caps: the omission of the cap design in the first description, the definite article in the second description, and the emphasis on the painted label in both. What is bothersome is that the modification in the wording of this label in the second description remains unexplained.

The answer to the question "who?" in mystery stories matches two sets of characteristics: the entity with characteristics a and b is the same individual as the entity with characteristics c and d. Explanations will show the compatibility of the two sets. But what provides the thrill of the denouement is the proper name. Its simplicity produces an effect similar to that of some algebraic equations: the individual who did x, y, z equals . . . Jones!

My "real" name may not indicate any physical or psychological trait. But I have been taught to consider it as if it were my substance. It masks and compensates for my lack of substance; it is myself, in a word. It functions like the mysterious substratum that some philosophers thought they had to postulate, as they despaired of making a set of properties or phenomena yield an individual. It may be—it would be if it were really "proper"—a permanent and unique characteristic.

Narrative fiction emphasizes the function of proper names, since the characters are pure creatures of language. Straight narratives use proper names in a straight fashion. They may also endow them with the descriptive or emblematic value of nicknames. Who-done-its or rather who-will-have-done-its further enhance the function of names: what is to be disclosed is, above all, a name. The emblematic value of names, if there is one, is sharpened; the name serves as a clue, possibly an ironical clue, like "Old Charley Goodfellow" in *Thou Art the Man*. But at the same time, hermeneutic tales are inclined to expose names as hollow idols, suggest that they mask a lack of substance instead of performing as straight or ironical emblems. Names remain necessary indexes of personified individuals. But assumptions of permanence and uniqueness are undermined. In Agatha Christie's *Peril at End House,* the solution hinges on the hidden fact that two characters share the same first name. A character may borrow someone else's name. Or he may use several names without having to resort to a physical disguise: the name is changed, not the description. Aliases allow the final revelation to assume a more stunning form. The equation "The individual who did x, y, z is Jones" becomes "Smith is Jones."

As noted in the section on destiny, *The Red Right Hand* exemplifies plays on names in a parodic fashion. It also uses another feature of language that does not correspond to a nonlinguistic feature: the diversity of languages. A house in France may resemble a house in England. But the words "house" and *maison* are quite different. The Latin meaning of "Dexter" is sufficiently hidden in *The Red Right Hand* to allow the adoption of this title in English. But a French translator might have to select *La Rouge Main Droite* over the more elegant *La Dextre Rouge* to avoid making the clue too transparent.

To the diversity of languages corresponds the diversity of synonymous or nearly equivalent words and phrases within one language: *maison* differs from "house," but so does "residence." A mystery story can conceal a duality by using the same terms to describe two individuals, human or not. Inversely, it can hide an identity by using different terms. Abusively perhaps, *The Chinese Orange Mystery* relies on an equivalence between "turned-round collar" and "clerical collar." Homonyms, or different pronunciations of the same word, are another means of concealment. In *The Gold Bug* Jupiter is quoted as saying "syphon" instead of "cipher." Among other semantic tricks, an unusual discrepancy between pronunciation and spelling plays a part in *The List of Adrian Messenger,* by Philip MacDonald, a text that lacks the literary quality of *The Red Right Hand* but whose parodic aspect is equally exemplary.

Adrian Messenger leaves a list of ten names with a Scotland Yard official. "The tale hinges, like so much in humanity's history, on a piece of paper." It also hinges on other linguistic factors. The dying "messenger" utters an enigmatic message that appears to contain two names. One, "Jocelyn," finds an easy reference. But the other, "Emma," resists interpretation until it is realized that "Emma's book" should be interpreted as "MS book." Inversely, what appears to be a common noun has to be interpreted as a proper name. Messenger's last words are reported by a Frenchman, St. Denis, whose English, like that of Poirot and other fictional characters, displays an odd distribution of ignorance and knowledge regarding idioms and vocabulary.[1] One of Messenger's words was "broom," followed by "clean sweep." St. Denis understood "broom" as *balai,* which he unaccountably retranslated as "brush." But "broom" is to be construed as "Bruttenholm." Before the main investigator, Anthony Gethryn, is enabled to go back from "brush" to "Bruttenholm," the reader has charitably been warned about the pronunciation of this noble name.

The murderer is a Bruttenholm. He has set out to eliminate those who might prevent him from inheriting the title and the estate. It will be revealed that his official name is a deformation of "Bruttenholm": "Brougham." Since this is not a sufficient disguise, the murderer also assumes other names, a new one for each new operation. The murderer is not the only character with more than one name. Gethryn's *nom de guerre* was "Polidor," that of St. Denis was "Ajax." The wife of one of the victims, Lady Pomfret, has become Mrs. Kouroudjian. Inversely, "J. Slattery" is the name of two characters, a fact that causes a delay in the investigation. The pen names of authors of newspaper articles are dutifully mentioned.

The story extends the French-English motif beyond the crucial Bruttenholm-broom-*balai*-brush imbroglio. Just before he receives Messenger's last message, St. Denis happens to wonder whether "braces" (or "suspenders") is the British (or American) translation of *bretelles.* Not only St. Denis but also Gethryn sprinkle their speech with French words. The motif of the cryptic message is picked up in an allusion to coded communications during the war between Gethryn in London and St. Denis in France. And Gethryn, in order to trap the murderer, will leak information to the press concerning the whereabouts of the last individual the murderer still has to kill.

Artificial ciphers, based on special codes, are not so

well suited to mystery stories as cryptic formulas that are content to exploit poetic resources such as homonymy and metaphor. Messenger's last words make no apparent sense. Instead of this, a cryptogram may develop a fairly simple homology between apparent and concealed meanings. It then provides a concentrated image of the relation between investigative sequence and investigated events.

In Leblanc's *La Comtesse de Cagliostro,* the first letters of the words in a key sentence yield "Alcor," an Arabic word that is said to mean "test" and names a minor star in Ursa Major. The major stars are arranged in the same configuration as the major Norman abbeys north of the Seine. A sky-earth homology is also to be found in one of Mallarmé's sonnets. Three main topics can be extracted from it: a swan *(cygne)* on a frozen lake, Cygnus *(Cygne)* against the background of the Milky Way, and a sign *(signe)* on a white page. In the poem, the sky-earth homology is based on homonyms, whereas in Leblanc's story, it is the geometric design that matters. This is an accidental difference. The essential difference is that the sonnet fuses the meanings in such a way that an asymmetric distinction between apparent and concealed, between what symbolizes and what is symbolized cannot be made. In the story, on the other hand, the stellar meaning of "Alcor" is the clue to the location of a treasure. Unlike a hermetic poem, a hermeneutic tale has to privilege a target meaning.

*From mystery stories
to pseudonarratives*

MYSTERY STORIES set up a narrative problem within a narrative. Whether or not the trouble is reflected in fictional psychology (amnesia, double personality, errors of perception), the stories depict a narrative illness that is finally cured. This raises the question: what if it were not cured? In this final section I shall be concerned with texts that may be viewed as deriving from this question. I must note at the outset that a narrative illness is not necessarily an esthetic deficiency. Let us recall in particular that lyric poetry endeavors to make its logic triumph at the expense of prosaic logics (narrative, analytic, dramatic) and of their master molds (individuation, classification, personification).

Anthony Berkeley's *The Poisoned Chocolates Case* and Cameron McCabe's *The Face on the Cutting-Room Floor* are examples of texts that depart from the constitutive convention of one final crystallization. They give several answers to the narrative question and avoid making a definite decision. The alternative is no answer at all. Some texts adopt this strategy. Stories like Franz Kafka's *Der Prozess* or Maurice Blanchot's *Aminadab* leave a question unanswered in the reader's mind, but it is primarily the question *why* rather than *who, what, when,* or *how.* Surrealistic narratives include odd and fantastic elements, but they do not present them as clues or masks, as raising a problem. Stories like *L'Emploi du Temps* and *Degrés* by Michel Butor, or *La Mise en Scène,* by Claude Ollier, are more closely related to hermeneutic tales. They project a sequence that looks like an investigative sequence yet does not result in a determination of the problematic events.

Mystery stories can extend the narrative trouble to primary carriers of the viewpoint. These characters are not allowed to tell definite lies, but they may be the victims of errors of perception, amnesia, or schizophrenia. Some of their thoughts may be concealed. In Christie's *The Murder of Roger Ackroyd,* the narrator deliberately conceals some events. In Rogers's *The Red Right Hand,* the flood of coincidences and correspondences and the evocation of various episodes through a narratively dislocated monologue combine to blur the vision of a sequence and the distinction between investigative and investigated events. If we remove the denouement, *The Red Right Hand,* published in 1945, may be regarded as a forerunner of texts that set a literary fashion in France in the 1950s. These texts are basically inconsistent to the extent that they are narrative.

Some of these texts are dramatic scripts. In *La Cantatrice Chauve,* by Eugène Ionesco, two characters infer from coincidences that they must have been living together as man and wife. Enters a maid, who "demonstrates" that they are wrong and who reveals that her "real" name is "Sherlock Holmes." In *En attendant Godot,* by Samuel Beckett, the name "Godot" is the source of a problem of individuation that will not be solved. It also remains undecided whether two messengers are one individual or not. *Autour de Mortin,* by Robert Pinget, consists of a series of testimonies that conflict in such a way that one may wonder whether they are about the same individual. In *Le Professeur Taranne,* by Arthur Adamov, it is the protagonist who loses his identity; everything that he claims about himself, including his name, is contradicted by other characters. These works are reminiscent of Pirandello, in particular of *Cosi è (se vi pare),* in which a woman refuses to choose between incompatible stories that her husband and her mother told about her.

A text that is designed to be performed relies on actors and props fully to project a fictional process. It is not necessary for the spoken sentences themselves to be narratively coherent for this effect to be achieved. If the text is only read, a rudimentary fictional sequence can be imagined, thanks to stage directions and to the names of the characters who address each other. Dramas in which the characters do not narrate show that narrative language is an unnecessary crutch. The dramatic scripts I have mentioned adopt the opposite tactic: narrative propositions cancel one another. Systematic narrative inconsistency in a dramatic work has no deeper effect than an unsolved narrative problem in a consistent story. For in a drama, spatiotemporal coherence does not depend on the content of narrative sentences.

The case of narratively inconsistent texts that cannot pass for dramatic scripts is quite different. In the absence of a dramatic base, one may simply be left with a story-like bunch of sentences that constitute neither one story nor several autonomous stories. The stylistic devices that writers of hermeneutic tales developed to keep some axioms in suspense are borrowed to prevent not only the investigated events but also the investigative sequence from crystallizing. The generalized failure of individuation dissolves all characters, including the carrier of the viewpoint.

Le Voyeur, by Alain Robbe-Grillet, still allows the reader roughly to project a sequence and to recognize "Mathias" as the name of a character whose viewpoint is most often adopted. However, it remains undecided whether some evocations are to be projected as perceptions, dreams, or memories of Mathias. This character is reminiscent of the daydreaming Beaumont in Pierre Véry's *Les Quatre Vipères* or of the acutely schizophrenic Hungerford in Helen Eustis's *The Horizontal Man.* But, in *Le Voyeur,* there is no retroactive denouement.

In *La Jalousie* and *Dans le labyrinthe,* also by Robbe-Grillet, the establishment of a fictional process is more systematically kept in check. *Dans le labyrinthe* begins with the sentence: "I am alone here now." The meaning of these three shifters (I, here, now) will not be satisfactorily filled. The reader may have the impression that "I" designates a character who tries to reconstruct events that took place in the town outside the room where he is now. But unlike Harry Riddle in *The Red Right Hand,* such a character would not manage to tie the episodes he evokes into a coherent process. Besides, this interpretation would be based on the assumption that a shoe box in the room is the same individual object as a shoe box that appears in the imagined episodes. This hypothesis is undermined by the fact that the relations between other objects in the room and objects in the town episodes are clearly analogical. For instance, dust corresponds to snow and the scene represented in a painting serves as a model for a café scene. The reader may consequently be inclined to switch to another interpretation: the character designated by "I" would not try to reconstruct past events; he would simply dream imaginary scenes, using the objects he perceives in his room as springboards. But this second interpretation is undermined by the fact that there is no clear stylistic distinction between what is perceived and what is imagined. The dream-like status of the town episodes contaminates the room episodes. Analogies become confusions. An object in the room fails to be properly identified; instead of an individuating label, such as "the paper-knife," the text provides only metaphorical predicates: "dagger," "flower," "human figure." And the first-person pronoun itself, which appears only at the beginning and at the end of the text, does not firmly situate a character somewhere at a certain time. The town episodes feature something called "the soldier." But since these episodes do not constitute a coherent sequence of imagined events, the repetitions of this label project a soldierly figure rather than one or several individuals. *Dans le labyrinthe* is reminiscent of *The Red Right Hand,* but unlike the French text, *The Red Right Hand* proves to be a hermeneutic tale: individuation finally triumphs over metaphor. The evocations of the hitchhiker, for instance, crystallize into the identification of two distinct individuals.

Texts by Claude Ollier (other than *La Mise en Scène*) and by Claude Simon (for instance, *La Route des Flandres*) would furnish other examples of pseudonarratives published in the 1950s and later. Simon borrows devices from William Faulkner and pushes them to extremes: loose, interminable sentences that pretend to aim at descriptive precision and manage instead to disintegrate object and event in a flood of properties and metaphors. *L'Innommable,* by Samuel Beckett, concentrates the interest on the first-person pronoun. Various attempts to develop what it may designate cancel one another. This text thus may be likened to Arthur Adamov's *Le Professeur Taranne.* But *L'Innommable* adopts the aspect of a rumination, not of a dramatic dialogue that could be staged. This produces a different effect.[2]

These pseudonarratives bear a negative relation both to hermeneutic tales and to straight stories. They dissolve narration into descriptions, individuals into properties, subjects into predicates, incompatibilities into contrasts. Since the Symbolist period at least, it has become clear that a poetic meaning can emanate from a set of disjointed narrative evocations. If the last pages of *The Red Right Hand,* in which a narrative meaning crystallizes, were removed, this mystery story would turn into a lengthy prose poem. This is the perspective of interpretation and appreciation that I would be inclined to adopt toward most of the pseudonarratives I mentioned. The following question may be asked: can poetic correspondences provide long texts with a sufficient structure? *L'Innommable,* on the other hand, is concerned with the philosophical topic of selfhood; it turns Descartes's *Méditations* into an anti-Cartesian rumination. Here again, one may wonder why the text is so long.

On the whole, commentators have so far avoided

viewing these texts as prose poems or ruminative essays. They have docilely accepted the label "novel" *(roman)*, under which these texts were often published. Emulating Joan of Arc, some critics have intimated that, while they read, they heard narrative "voices." If one possesses this kind of gift, reading any kind of text must be like listening to a dramatic performance on the radio. In any case, the word "novel," conveniently undefined, has served to stress the difference between these texts and stories, either hermeneutic or straight, and veil their similarity with prose poems. In part at least, the preference that critics generally have shown for pseudonarratives over mystery stories seems to stem from the fact that the absence of narrative crystallization makes the interpretative task more radical and provides greater opportunity for delightful controversy. Hermeneutic denouements are supposed to "reassure" the reader, and for some time, quite a few commentators have deemed it proper to frown upon texts that they feel are designed to reassure or, more simply, tell an "anecdote" (that is to say, make narrative sense).[3]

The label "phenomenological" has been used to characterize pseudonarratives. "Phenomenalistic" may be more appropriate, however. A philosopher who adopts a phenomenological approach may or may not develop a phenomenalistic ontology and epistemology. In philosophical discussions, "phenomenalism" is generally opposed to "realism" in one or two senses of this polysemic word. Phenomenalists consider sensory phenomena as basic entities. Such phenomena are not events; they have spatial and temporal aspects or mean-

ings, but they are not situated. According to phenomenalists, individuals are constructed out of or signified by
phenomena. Some realists, on the other hand, see individuals as basic entities. If they are Platonists, they
privilege classes of individuals.

The phenomena with which phenomenalists are concerned are sensory signals rather than linguistic signs. If
the issue is transferred to a linguistic plane, a language
like English may be said to favor some kind of realism
since it classifies and individuates directly, signifying individuals and classes of individuals ("George," "a man,"
"man") without having to develop descriptions of sensory phenomena. Such descriptions are normally carried
by predicates subordinated to subjects. Straight narratives individuate as a matter of course. They would thus
be logically "realistic" whether they project fictional or
historical individuals and whether or not they resort to
"realistic" devices that tend to foster a confusion between fiction and history.

These two senses of "realistic" would go together if
it were decreed that only historical entities can properly
be said to be individuals, hence that a narrative is either
historical or produces an illusion of historicity. This position would be countenanced by a philosophical tradition which takes truth as the linguistic goal *par excellence.*
Fictionalizing narratives, whose indications are neither
true nor false, would thus be deprived of an autonomous
status. This assumption has made its influence felt in
esthetics. It has resulted in the uncomfortable theory of
art as illusory and yet somehow capable of "truth." To
my way of thinking, if there is an illusion it is the illusion

produced by the theory itself. Truth is only one linguistic value among others; it is the value to be sought in historicizing language, which is only one mode of meaning among others. Art is "lusion" (*i.e.,* play), not illusion. By itself, narrative logic is not oriented toward history more than toward fiction. The commentators and the authors of pseudonarratives, however, have not adopted this outlook. They seem to have assumed that coherent narrative fiction could only be an illusory ersatz of historical reports and that, if "the novel" were to be given an autonomous status, the attack against "realism" would have to be directed not only against what I called "legend" but also against the logic of space, time, and individuals, that is to say, the logic of narration itself.

Insofar as it tries to make sense out of verbal phenomena without individuating or classifying, poetry might be said to have "phenomenalistic" aspirations. But while phenomenalistic philosophers try to schematize the construction of individuals out of phenomenal material, poets endeavor to extricate experiences of purely verbal phenomena out of a stubbornly individuating and classifying language. Hermeneutic tales would be "realistic" to the extent that, like straight narratives, they individuate without any fuss. But they are also concerned with problems of individuation, which bear some correspondence to the difficulties that phenomenalists encounter as they attempt to show how phenomena can yield coherent individuation. Pseudonarratives illustrate absences of individuation. They might thus be said to be "phenomenalistic" in a poetic sense. But if these absences are stressed as failures, pseudonarratives might be labelled "antiphenomenalistic," because they would seem to deny the phenomenalistic thesis that phenomena provide sufficient clues for coherent individuation.

Of course, this is only a semblance. For someone who plays with words, to individuate or not is simply a matter of choosing between modes of meaning, between basic styles. To the extent that, unlike straightforward poems, inconclusive investigations and pseudonarratives cultivate the impression that they have the same goal as hermeneutic tales, they systematize the kind of coquettishness with which lengthening devices used in mystery stories may be taxed. In the case of inconclusive investigations, it is not the denouement that is postponed, it is the absence of a denouement altogether. In the case of pseudonarratives, the whole text remains narratively inconsistent.

Epilogue

MYSTERY STORIES have not escaped critical and scholarly attention; histories of the genre have been published. But histories of literature at large have so far considered the genre as marginal.

Reviewers of mystery stories usually refrain from disclosing the denouement. It might be alleged that this scruple has impeded precise textual analysis. Or it might be said that the particular interest that mystery stories are designed to stimulate on first reading has led to the sweeping inference that none was worth rereading. I did not make this inference. As far as my tastes and experience go, the proportion of esthetically worthless texts in the field of mystery stories is no higher than in any other area. None of the mystery stories I have read is esthetically impeccable, but I should say the same for any kind of text.

In order to develop esthetic considerations, I have delimited my topic according to form. One of my purposes was to show how hermeneutic stories illustrate aspirations and difficulties specific to narrative art. I laid aside mystery plays and films because their medium is not purely linguistic, and I devoted more attention to long stories because longer texts are better tests of narrative art.

In critical and historical studies, the hermeneutic genre has often been masked by one of its possible contents: a detective who finally triumphs over a hidden opponent. A stress on content is likely to draw the attention away from basic semantic and esthetic questions. To the extent that the topic can be discussed in esthetic terms, I myself have expressed some misgivings about the detective-versus-murderer pattern. It is also to be noted that writers of detective stories have often made the same detective reappear again and again in subsequent books. In so doing, they have incited their readers to achieve an intimacy with the character or the figure rather than with particular texts; such readers thus enjoy returning to the same character instead of rereading the same text.

But the relevancy of these considerations is compromised by a misleading postulate. In the foregoing paragraphs, I have proceeded as if literary criticism derived essentially from a desire to formulate one's esthetic tastes coherently and as if, consequently, the low ranking of hermeneutic tales or of detective stories testified to a consensus of elaborated tastes. In view of the variety of temperaments and experiences, it would be perverse to assume even the possibility of such a consensus. And, in any case, resemblances between ratings on the literary stock exchange and the tastes of real persons, living or dead, are purely coincidental. How else could it be? Rankings of authors, texts, or types of texts reflect the amount of critical talk more than the content of critical judgments. Besides, these judgments themselves are often warped by a desire or a practical necessity to assume a certain kind of role in the critical Babel. Reactions to other critics insidiously or deliberately alter and smother reactions to what one is supposed to be talking about. Collective agreements about what constitutes "serious literature," about "greatness" and "importance," or about what is major and what is minor manifest a somewhat hypocritical and self-hypocritical, cultural or countercultural religiosity according to tradition, fashion, or political dictates. If the low ranking of mystery stories or detective stories is to be discussed at all, it had better be considered as a convention, not as a consensus of tastes.

It would not do to attribute this low ranking to an official snobbishness regarding "popular" literature in general; mystery stories have recruited their readers from all classes and milieux. Some consecrated writers have expressed their esteem for the genre, others have written mystery stories among other things. To propose as a sufficient explanation this very lack of discriminatory appeal would not do, either, since the same remark would apply to some of the texts established as "great." One might emphasize an incompatibility between the physicalistic bias of mystery stories and a cultural spiritualism that feeds upon individuated spirits (persons, souls) or collective spirits (social classes, political movements, nations, mankind). But what about the positivistic trend? It might be claimed that positivists do not make their influence felt on literary rankings.

The enhancement of the ludic interest that mystery stories cultivate suggests another reason. This characteristic would be looked at askance, not because it would be considered detrimental to esthetic endurance but because it would compromise socioreligious seriousness. This kind of seriousness attempts to avoid both ludic earnestness and moral gravity by confusing the two. But cultural religiosity, like some polytheistic cults, has shown great digestive powers, at least in the Western zone. Rabelais has long been canonized and the procedure of beatification is on its way for Dadaists and Surrealists. Perhaps we should push a little further. The enhancement of the ludic interest goes with the constitution of mystery stories as a recognizable genre. I find the following hypothesis attractive: if mystery stories have so far generally been considered as a minor or marginal genre, it may be, in part at least, because they do look like a genre; and more precisely because, unlike odes or sonnets, epics or tragedies, they developed as a genre at the wrong time.

In order to look "serious," histories of literature are inclined to aim at unity on two levels. They have to resemble one another in order to look like History. And each of them has to select, conceal, hierarchize, and compose its material so as to give the impression that an evolutionary process takes charge of various authors, works, and movements. The esthetic coherence of an *Entwicklungsroman* thus becomes confused with the cognitive principle of the unity of the historical field. If literature is to be viewed as one process during the nineteenth and twentieth centuries, at least in the Western zone, what can most easily pass for a general trend? Expression, revolt, experimentation may be emphasized, but they will not provide an evolutionary principle unless they are shown to result in the dissolution of genres rather than in the creation of new ones. This entropic progress may even be regarded as applying to literature itself, not just to genres. Nowadays, quite a few critics take it for granted that literature is "dead" unless, of course, criticism itself should be taken as a literary genre.

Some, perhaps most, critics and historians still make use of genre labels. But these labels are not based on a typology of semantic modes. Distinctions between kinds of novels, for instance, convey the impression of attempting to define the species of an undefined genus. It seems to be generally assumed that novels have a narrative aspect. But texts that are essentially dialogues have been tagged "novels." Proust's main work, in which an essayistic style takes precedence over narrative, has received the same label. In the case of pseudonarratives, the assumption that the narrative aspect of a novel should be coherent is dropped. Many critical essays are content to consider novels as sociological and psychological studies. Chesterton's judgment regarding the inability of mystery stories to develop into "novels" echoes this approach. What, then, is a novel these days? As far as I can see, a fairly long text, in prose, which is not designed for dramatic performances, whose indications are not subject to verification, and which has to be neither narratively nor philosophically coherent qualifies as a novel. This raises questions: what makes the work one text? And if some kind of coherence or cohesiveness should be felt, what makes the text a "novel" rather than, say, a "prose poem," if one insists on using these labels?

If the dissolution of genres is implicitly or explicitly chosen as the evolutionary principle that alone can tie together various considerations about nineteenth-century and twentieth-century literature, then mystery stories will appear "reactionary." More precisely, the retroactive denouement that I took to be specific to hermeneutic tales will represent a reactionary, some would say "reassuring," attempt to rescue the narrative mode of meaning *in extremis.* The irony would be that the attempt to select and arrange historical facts so as to make them look like one process testifies to a need for a narrative kind of logic. Whether they deal with literature or not, histories may even recall hermeneutic tales to the extent that the present state of affairs, as the historian is pleased to interpret it, is bound to function implicitly as a retroactive denouement. Did historians of literature feel that mystery stories threatened to make literary history appear as a game, hence as not "serious"?

Mystery stories can also provide a skeptical comment on this epilogue. I have avoided committing myself to a panoramic vision of the recent evolution of literature. Still, in order to stress a cultural convention, I did engage in the game of selecting and simplifying somewhat nebulous historical facts. And my surmises regarding motives may be likened to the comments of a fictional detective adorning his solution with an answer to the question *why.* It is easy to invent and apply motives: pick one, and any kind of behavior can be interpreted as either expression or concealment. But unlike a fictional detective or a psychoanalyst, I cannot propose to force a corroborative statement out of the murderer.

Appendix

THE PARADOXICAL CASE OF
DOCTOR FELL

I do not love thee, Doctor Fell.
The reason why I cannot tell:
But this alone I know full well:
I do not love thee, Doctor Fell.

ANONYMOUS

IN A CHAPTER OF *The Three Coffins,* Doctor Gideon Fell classifies locked-room problems. There are also "locked rooms" in philosophy. Their "topology" is not spatial, but philosophers are wont to resort to images: the Platonic cave pictures the human condition, Wittgenstein's bottle, the philosophic condition. The preamble of Doctor Fell's lecture can be used to introduce a philosophical locked-room puzzle:

> "I will now lecture," said Dr. Fell inexorably, "on the general mechanics and development of the situation which is known in detective fiction as the 'hermetically sealed chamber'. Harrumph. All those opposing can skip this chapter. Harrumph. To begin with, gentlemen!

Having been improving my mind with sensational fiction
for the last forty years, I can say—"

"But, if you're going to analyze impossible situations," interrupted Pettis, "why discuss detective
fiction?"

"Because," said the doctor, frankly, "we're in a detective story, and we don't fool the reader by pretending
we're not. Let's not invent excuses to drag in a discussion of detective stories. Let's candidly glory in the nobl-
est pursuits possible to characters in a book."

Doctor Fell, who is confronted with a locked-room
puzzle and is about to lecture about this kind of enigma,
appears to have locked himself up in the fictional field.
He says in effect that he is a fictional character. This is
a refreshing shift for a reader who has grown tired of
characters in novels who claim that they are not in a
novel or who reflect that the adventure they are living is
like fiction, hence that it is not fiction. This happens in
mystery stories as often as elsewhere. The case of Doctor
Fell is much rarer, though it is not unique; one might
think of Pirandello, for instance. Doctor Fell's fictional
cogito looks like a self-fictionalizing statement, that is to
say, a statement that would characterize itself as a
fictional speech event.

If a text is interpreted as a piece of narrative fiction,
its propositions are implicitly bound by a fictionalizing
operator that, *from the outside,* bears on all the events that
the propositions project. Sometimes this operator is formulated in a preliminary warning: "All the characters in

this book are fictitious." A declaration like that of Doctor Fell appears to transfer the fictionalizing operator inside the fiction and thus to make it immanent.

If I interpret a statement in a historicizing perspective, I assume that it occurs in the spatiotemporal field where I embody myself and where my interpretative activity also takes place as an event or process, among others. Thus the historicizing operator historicizes itself; by nature, it would seem to be immanent. On the contrary, if I approach a narrative as a piece of fiction, I do not place myself and my interpretative activity in the field of the narrated events.

English does not reserve a special morphology, syntax, or vocabulary for fictionalizing purposes. Hence it is possible to interpret the same narrative as history (true or false) or fiction (neither true nor false). Stylistic features may help or hamper the decision. Realistic devices appear designed to blur the distinction between history and fiction. I called "legend" a confusion between the two. Letting a character in a novel assert that he is not a character in a novel would be such a device, similar to an intimate mixture of fictional elements with geographical and historical details. This pseudohistorical cogito would be a legendary cogito.

Doctor Fell acknowledges "frankly" that he is "in a detective story." Unlike a legendary cogito, his statement seems to confirm the distinction between historical and fictional. But it threatens to blur this distinction in another way. Is not the doctor allowed to usurp a privilege of self-recognition that should be reserved for the historical cogito? If the fictionalizing operator is permitted to become immanent, how can it be philosophically distinguished from a historicizing operator?

One might try to limit the scope of Doctor Fell's assertion by interpreting it as follows: "Right now, I am in a detective story, but basically, I am as real as the reader to whom I allude." An actor could say: "I am Hamlet," meaning that he plays the role of Hamlet, that he is Hamlet only fictionally. Attributed to the actor, not to the character, the fictionalizing operator would thus recover its transcendence. But, to apply this tactic to Doctor Fell, one would have to consider him as a historical individual playing the role of a character with the same name. The text as a whole does not urge me to distinguish a historical Fell from a fictional Fell. The result of this first attempt at unraveling the paradox would rather be to reduce the self-fictionalizing cogito to a legendary cogito. Doctor Fell would insinuate that his existence is not limited to the fictional field. But this existence would not be historical, for I do not have at my disposal any piece of external information that would incline me to historicize Doctor Fell.

If his existence is accepted as merely fictional, cannot we at least distinguish between two levels of fiction? In *Hamlet*, there is a play within the play; in some novels, a character writes a novel. This situation allows a first-level fictional statement to declare that the events on the second level are fictional. But the text of *The Three Coffins* excludes the possibility of distinguishing between two levels of fiction. Doctor Fell is not like a character who, during an episode, would play the detective in a murder game. His statement is reminiscent of that best-known of philosophical paradoxes, the Paradox of the Liar, with the exception that it appears to fictionalize itself instead of falsifying itself.

But cannot we simply view the lecturing Fell as a fictional representative of the author? Is it not enough to regard his cogito as an ironical allusion to characters who claim that they are real individuals? And is not the irony intended to bear on the declaration itself as an excuse? A character who says he is in a detective story does not make a lecture on detective stories more natural, especially if the lecture seems to refer to stories that were published at a certain historical time in a geographical place. Is not the most appropriate tactic the reduction of Doctor Fell's words to a reflection, in the fictional field, of thoughts to be attributed to the author or to the reader?

This trivialization of the phenomenon allows one to explain the paradoxical effect as a mirage. Doctor Fell remains confined to his fictional world, and the fictionalizing operator is pulled out of it; only the operator's reflection is to be attributed to the character. The spell due to its grammatical dependence on a first-person pronoun would thus be broken. After all, what happens in a fictional field is always, through quotation or description, simply a projection of the thoughts of author and readers. What is special about Doctor Fell's case is simply that it echoes a thought that underlies all others, namely the sustained decision to interpret the text as narrative fiction, not as historical report.

But what prevents us from applying this treatment of Doctor Fell's fictional cogito to the historical cogito? Cannot the immanence of the latter be similarly regarded as a grammatical mirage? Is not the inscription of the historicizing operator as a mental *event* in the historical field to be interpreted as the projected image of an *act* that transcends this field?

It is even tempting to push the similarity further, to reduce what is imagined to what is imaginary and to reduce the opposition between history and fiction to a relation between two fictional levels. All the world would be a stage and all the men and women merely "players." We would be characters in a comedy, a tragedy, an epic, a picaresque novel, or a detective story, with or without a divine detective.

I recognize the transcendence of the historicizing operator and accept the ontological depreciation of the historical mode of existence that goes with it. What is basic is what is felt. What is felt is qualitative; it is not individuated. What is felt is actual, but its actuality is not ordered according to a spatiotemporal logic. Events are reflections of acts. I am a historical individual: I am made up of events and it is only as an event that the historicizing operator can be attributed to me.

But this move does not entail a reduction of imagined to imaginary and of history to basic fiction. There is more than a difference of degree between Doctor Fell on the one hand and the reader or the author on the other. The plurality of the metaphors to which I alluded shows that they are only esthetic metaphors, more or less revealing and misleading according to mood, circumstances, and temperament. Is the historicizing "text," whose grammar natural science tries to establish, a comedy, a tragedy, an epic, a mystery story?

There are epics, mystery stories, dramas. But though there are many books of history, there is only one historical field. Between pieces of fiction there are resemblances and differences. Between historical reports there are agreements and contradictions. The existence of Doctor Fell is projected by the interpretation of homogeneous signs in limited number. My historical existence is projected by the interpretation of heterogeneous signs in practically unlimited number. Semiotic heterogeneity is one of the conditions of the possibility of truth. An art, a genre, or a particular text limit the number and nature of their signs. Any signifying act, on the contrary, can be projected as a historical event.

This ontological strategy is not Cartesian. The Cartesian cogito places not only the signifying act (called "thinking") but also the ego outside the locked room of history. On the transcendental level, the cogito attributes thinking to the ego. Why? "It is so obvious that it is I who doubt, who understand, and who desire, that there is no need of adding any explanation." This impression of evidence absorbs the following postulates: 1. Doubting, thinking, and desiring imply an entity that doubts, thinks, and desires; in other words, these verbs are not like "to rain." 2. This entity should be personified; these verbs demand a personified subject. 3. An experience of the Cartesian type involves only one such entity. 4. The first-person pronoun is an appropriate index for this entity.

What is felt has a first-person aspect, an aspect of self versus not-self. But this aspect is qualitative and varies according to experiences, according to work and play, pain and pleasure, ordinary or mystical experiences. In a painful experience, the active aspect is in conflict with the first-person aspect. In a Cartesian experience, among others, the two aspects are allied: thinking is experienced in conjunction with selfhood. But the formula "I think, therefore I am" is not content to say this. It involves a personification and also, in my opinion, an individuation: "I am thinking, therefore I am a personified individual."

The Cartesian strategy manifests a tendency to separate personification from individuation: an individual is a body; a person or persona is a spirit. The hypothesis of the evil genius, who is not situated, contributes to the effect. The Trickster systematizes errors regarding bodies, but a personified deceiver personifies the deceived entity. It must be acknowledged that the principle of identity is not the same for persons and individuals. But personification cannot dispense with individuation, even if the latter is limited to a voice occurring somewhere at a certain time, as in the case of Joan of Arc and her angels.

In fact, there is a passage in Descartes's *Méditations* that temporalizes the ego explicitly: "*I am, I exist:* this is certain; but how long? As long as I keep thinking." The text thus seems to foreshadow the Bergsonian equation of spirituality with time and of materiality with space. But how can there be succession without concomitance and concomitance without spatiality? If the temporal nature of the ego is not in doubt, then its spatial nature is not in doubt. What can be questioned is the place it occupies in a spatial and temporal field. But this is an epistemological not an ontological issue. The *Méditations* tend to confuse the two.

In *The Three Coffins,* a trickster uses a mirror to produce a locked-room illusion inside the fiction. To unravel the paradox of Doctor Fell's words, I have resorted to a mirror metaphor. Personified individuals have been confined to the realm of tricky reflections. A grammatical reflection transposes the experience of thinking with a first-person quality into an individual who is thinking. These "reflections" recall the "shadows" in the Platonic cave. But transtemporal acts supplant intemporal forms. And unlike a demiurgic activity, these acts are not personified.

Philosophical detection bears some resemblance to fictional detection. My conclusion is not cognitive; it can be neither true nor false. And though the style is analytic, the conclusion is not analytically necessary. But unlike what a fictional detective is empowered to proclaim, it does not enjoy the status of a narrative axiom. The reader is invited to play philosophical detective, according to his own tastes, with and within the maze of first-person mirrors.

In a way, Doctor Fell's statement appears to integrate

free comments of the dear-reader-our-heroine type within the fictional world. But according to my analysis, this integration is only a semblance. Doctor Fell's cogito reflects the fictionalizing operator that, in itself, must remain outside the fiction. As it is rarer and less stale, a statement like that of Doctor Fell has more piquancy but no more "body" than the dear-reader-our-heroine device.

Notes

Part I / Mystery

1. According to Boileau and Narcejac, in *Le Roman policier*, "if the detective novel exists, it is because, by means of fiction, the world can be questioned, the real can be decomposed and lost." If by "the world" one means semantic rules of individuation, this judgment concerns stories that foster an impression of impossibility. But it also can be applied to hermeneutic tales in general, insofar as they do not take for granted the composition of complex individuals out of events.

2. In *The Three Coffins* (British title: *The Hollow Man*), John Dickson Carr lets Doctor Fell declare: "It seems reasonable to point out that the word improbable is the very last which should ever be used to curse detective fiction in any case. A great part of our liking for detective fiction is based on a liking for improbability." Similarly, Marjorie Nicolson, in her essay, "The Professor and the Detective," says: "The charm of the pure detective story lies in its utter unreality." On the other hand, Raymond Chandler, in his "Casual Notes on the Mystery Novel," decides that, in order to insure credibility, a mystery story "must be about real people in a real world." In "The Simple Art of Murder," he takes exception to the behavior of some characters in the genteel kind of detective story: "When they did unreal things, they ceased to be real themselves." And he draws a

puzzling distinction between "real fiction" and "unreal fiction." If "real" means "authentic," should not authentic fiction distance itself as much as possible from narratives about historical reality?

3. In "Crime and Detection," E. M. Wrong claims that the detective story "seeks to justify the law and bring retribution to the guilty." According to Chandler in his "Casual Notes," "The mystery novel must punish the criminal in one way or another, not necessarily by operation of the law courts. Contrary to popular belief, this has nothing to do with morality. It is part of the logic of the form. Without this the story is like an unresolved chord in music. It leaves a sense of irritation." This passage is all the more baffling to me since I fail to see what kind of punishment is dealt in some of Chandler's own stories, such as *The Big Sleep, The High Window, The Little Sister,* or *Spanish Blood.*

4. In *The Tragedy of Birlstone,* Watson says that the sole reward for Holmes is "the intellectual joy of the problem." Yet Holmes pays at least lip service to social conventions: "I go into a case to help the ends of justice and the work of the police." In *The Quick One,* Chesterton's detective, Father Brown, declares: "I've never had anything to do with setting police machinery at work, or running down criminals, or anything like that." Actually, whether he piously closes his eyes or not, Father Brown's activities often result in trapping a criminal.

5. In Christie's *Murder at the Vicarage,* a doctor is allowed to say: "Shut up these people where they can't do any harm—even put them peacefully out of the way—yes, I'd go as far as that. But don't call it punishment. Don't bring shame on them and their innocent families." In *The Greene Murder Case,* by S. S. Van Dine, the detective, Philo Vance, indulges in the game of personifying a social order: "If society were omniscient, Markham, it would have a right to sit in judgment. But society is ignorant and venomous, devoid of any trace of insight or understanding. It exalts knavery and worships stupidity. It crucifies the intelligent, and puts the diseased in dungeons. And, withal, it arrogates to itself the right and ability to analyze the subtle sources of what it calls 'crime', and to condemn to death all persons whose inborn and irresistible impulses it does not like. That's your sweet society, Markham—a pack of wolves watering at the mouth for victims on whom to vent its organized lust to kill and flay." Philo Vance's conception of wolves is conventionally unfair. He also forgets to note that, far from being crucified, he enjoys a life of leisure thanks to the

laws and police of "your sweet society." Instead of pointing this out, he promises Markham, a district attorney, to turn his "victim" over to him. Fortunately, the murderer will kill herself.

Part II / Story

1. There are many other ways in which a story can be fattened and a denouement delayed. In *Mortal Consequences*, Julian Symons notes one of them: "The mystery is prolonged by the obstinate refusal of the characters to reveal essential facts."

2. Dorothy Sayers emphasizes the question of the narrative viewpoint in "Detective Fiction: Origins and Development."

3. In *Mortal Consequences*, Julian Symons states that "everything that happens is as Maigret sees it, or as it is told to him." Actually, Simenon does not eliminate free comments altogether, and, in *La Tête d'un Homme*, the first episode adopts the point of view of another character.

4. For examples of functional plot diagrams, see Josée Dupuy, *Le Roman Policier;* Edgar Marsch, *Die Kriminalerzählung;* and Stanko Lasić, *Poetika Kriminlististčkog Romana.*

Part III / Cryptogram

1. In *The Little Sister,* Chandler uses a phony mixture of Spanish and English in a more satisfactory way: as a clue.

2. Several critics have noted connections between mystery stories and inconclusive investigations, or pseudonarratives. See, for instance, Jean Alter's "L'Enquête policière dans le Nouveau Roman," Hanna Charney's "Pourquoi le 'nouveau roman' policier?" Michael Holquist's "Whodunit and other questions: metaphysical detective stories in post-war fiction," Gerda Zeltner's "Robert Pinget et le roman policier," and Ludovic Janvier's *Une Parole exigeante.*

3. In *Les Récréants: Essai sur le roman policier,* Jean-Marie Poupart alludes to the discredit into which narrative art has fallen when he opines that mystery stories can contribute to a "reevaluation" of the narrative for the sake of the narrative despite their "oblique" technique. "Thanks to" might be more appropriate than "despite."

Works Cited

Adamov, Arthur. *Le Professeur Taranne*. In *Théâtre I* (Paris: Gallimard, 1953).

Alter, Jean. "L'Enquête policière dans le Nouveau Roman." In
Un Nouveau Roman? Edited by J. H. Matthews (Paris: Minard,
1964).

Aragon, Louis. *Le Paysan de Paris* (Paris: Gallimard, 1926).

Barthes, Roland. *S/Z* (Paris: Le Seuil, 1970).

Barzun, Jacques, and Taylor, Wendell Hertig. *A Catalogue of
Crime* (New York: Harper, 1971).

Beckett, Samuel. *En attendant Godot* (Paris: Minuit, 1952).

———. *L'Innommable* (Paris: Minuit, 1953).

Berkeley, Anthony. *The Poisoned Chocolates Case* (New York:
Doubleday, 1929).

———. *Trial and Error* (New York: Doubleday, 1937).

Blanchot, Maurice. *Aminadab* (Paris: Gallimard, 1942).

Boileau, Pierre. *Le Repos de Bacchus*. In *Chambres Closes* (Paris:
Club du Livre Policier, 1961).

Boileau, Pierre, and Narcejac, Thomas. *"Au bois dormant."* In
Le Mauvais Oeil (Paris: Denoel, 1956).

———. *D'entre les morts* (Paris: Denoel, 1954).

———. *La Poudrière* (Paris: Champs-Elysées, 1974).

———. *Le Secret d'Eunerville* (Paris: Champs-Elysées, 1973).

Breton, André. *Nadja* (Paris: Gallimard, 1928).

Burack, A. S., ed. *Writing Detective and Mystery Fiction* (Boston: The Writer, 1945).

Butor, Michel. *Degrés* (Paris: Gallimard, 1960).

———. *L'Emploi du Temps* (Paris: Minuit, 1956).

Caillois, Roger. *Puissances du Roman* (Marseille: Sagittaire, 1942).

Camus, Albert. *L'Etranger* (Paris: Gallimard, 1942).

Carr, John Dickson. *The Burning Court* (New York: Harper, 1937).

———. "The Grandest Game in the World." See Nevins.

———. *The Lost Gallows* (New York: Harper, 1931).

———. *The Three Coffins* (New York: Harper, 1935).

———. *To Wake the Dead* (New York: Harper, 1938).

Champigny, Robert. *Ontology of the Narrative* (The Hague: Mouton, 1972).

Chandler, Raymond. *The Big Sleep* (New York: Knopf, 1939).

———. "Casual Notes on the Mystery Novel." In *Raymond Chandler Speaking* (Boston: Houghton Mifflin, 1962).

———. *Farewell My Lovely* (New York: Knopf, 1940).

———. *The High Window* (New York: Knopf, 1942).

———. *The Lady in the Lake* (New York: Knopf, 1943).

———. *The Little Sister* (Boston: Houghton Mifflin, 1949).

———. *Spanish Blood.* In *The Simple Art of Murder* (Boston: Houghton Mifflin, 1950).

———. *The Simple Art of Murder*, ibid.

Charney, Hanna. "Pourquoi le 'nouveau roman' policier?" *French Review*, XLVI, 1 (October 1972).

Chesterton, Gilbert Keith. "A Defence of Detective Stories." In *The Defendant* (London: Johnson, 1901).

———. *The Father Brown Omnibus* (New York: Dodd, Mead, 1951).

———. "On Detective Novels." In *Generally Speaking* (London: Methuen, 1928).

Christie, Agatha. *And Then There Were None* (New York: Dodd, Mead, 1940).

————. *Dead Man's Folly* (New York: Dodd, Mead, 1956).

————. *Death Comes as the End* (London: Collins, 1945).

————. *Five Little Pigs* (London: Collins, 1942).

————. *Murder at the Vicarage* (New York: Dodd, Mead, 1930).

————. *Murder in the Calais Coach* (New York: Dodd, Mead, 1934).

————. *A Murder Is Announced* (London: Collins, 1950).

————. *The Murder of Roger Ackroyd* (New York: Dodd, Mead, 1926).

————. *Peril at End House* (London: Collins, 1932).

————. *The Seven Dials Mystery* (New York: Dodd, Mead, 1929).

————. *Thirteen at Dinner* (New York: Dodd, Mead, 1933).

Crispin, Edmund. *The Moving Toyshop* (London: Gollancz, 1946).

Dard, Frédéric. *Le Monte-Charge* (Paris: Fleuve Noir, 1961).

Descartes, René. *Méditations.* In *Oeuvres et Lettres* (Paris: Gallimard, 1953).

Dickson, Carr. *The Bowstring Murders* (New York: Morrow, 1933).

Dickson, Carter. *The Ten Teacups* (London: Heinemann, 1935).

————. *The White Priory Murders* (New York: Morrow, 1934).

Doyle, Arthur Conan. *Sherlock Holmes* (New York: Heritage, 1950).

Duerrenmatt, Friedrich. *Das Versprechen* (Zurich: Schifferli, 1958).

Dupuy, Josée. *Le Roman Policier* (Paris: Larousse, 1974).

Eustis, Helen. *The Horizontal Man* (New York: Harper, 1946).

Freeman, R. Austin. "The Art of the Detective Story." See Haycraft.

Hammett, Dashiell. *The Maltese Falcon* (New York: Knopf, 1930).

————. *Red Harvest* (New York: Knopf, 1929).

Haycraft, Howard, ed. *The Art of the Mystery Story* (New York: Simon & Schuster, 1946).

Holquist, Michael. "Whodunit and Other Questions: Metaphysical Detective Stories in Post-War Fiction." *New Literary*

History. III, no. 1 (Autumn 1971).

Ionesco, Eugène. *La Cantatrice Chauve.* In *Théâtre I* (Paris: Gallimard, 1954).

Janvier, Ludovic. *Une Parole exigeante: le nouveau roman* (Paris: Minuit, 1964).

Kafka, Franz. *Der Prozess* (Berlin: Die Schmiede, 1925).

Kemelman, Harry. *The Nine-Mile Walk* (New York: Putnam, 1967).

Knox, Ronald. "A Detective Story Decalogue." See Haycraft.

Lacassin, Francis. *Mythologie du Roman Policier* (Paris: Union Générale d'Editions, 1974).

Lasić, Stanko. *Poetika Kriminalističkog Romana* (Zagreb: Liber, 1973).

Leblanc, Maurice. *Les Aventures d'Arsène Lupin,* 8 vols. (Paris: Gallimard, 1961–1962).

Le Carré, John. *The Spy Who Came In from the Cold* (London: Gollancz, 1963).

Leroux, Gaston. *Le Mystère de la Chambre Jaune.* In *Rouletabille I* (Paris: Laffont, 1961).

――――. *Le Parfum de la Dame en Noir,* ibid.

Levin, Ira. *A Kiss before Dying* (New York: Simon & Schuster, 1953).

McCabe, Cameron. *The Face on the Cutting-Room Floor* (London: Gollancz, 1936).

MacDonald, Philip. *The List of Adrian Messenger* (New York: Doubleday, 1959).

――――. *The Rasp* (New York: Doubleday, 1925).

Mallarmé, Stéphane. *Oeuvres Complètes* (Paris: Gallimard, 1945).

Marsch, Edgar. *Die Kriminalerzählung* (München: Winkler, 1972).

Messac, Régis. *Le Detective Novel et l'influence de la pensée scientifique* (Paris: Champion, 1929).

Narcejac, Thomas. See Boileau.

Nevins, Francis M., Jr., ed. *The Mystery Writer's Art* (Bowling Green University Press, 1970).

Nicolson, Marjorie. "The Professor and the Detective." See Haycraft.

Ollier, Claude. *La Mise en Scène* (Paris: Minuit, 1958).

Pinget, Robert. *Autour de Mortin* (Paris: Minuit, 1958).

Pirandello, Luigi. *Cosi è (se vi pare)* (Milano: Mondadori, 1967).

Poe, Edgar Allan. "Charles Dickens." In *Literary Criticism* (Boston: Estes, n.d.).

———. *Tales of Mystery and Imagination* (New York: Everyman, 1966).

Poupart, Jean-Marie. *Les Récréants* (Montréal: Le Jour, 1972).

Queen, Ellery. *And on the Eighth Day* (New York: Random House, 1964).

———. *The Chinese Orange Mystery* (New York: International Readers League, 1934).

———. *The Scarlet Letters* (Boston: Little, Brown, 1953).

———. *There Was an Old Woman* (Boston: Little, Brown, 1943).

Quincey, Thomas de. "Murder as One of the Fine Arts." In *Collected Writings*, XIII (London: Black, 1897).

Robbe-Grillet, Alain. *Dans le labyrinthe* (Paris: Minuit, 1959).

———. *La Jalousie* (Paris: Minuit, 1957).

———. *Le Voyeur* (Paris: Minuit, 1955).

Rogers, Joel Townsley. *The Red Right Hand* (New York: Simon & Schuster, 1945).

Ross, Barnaby. *The Tragedy of X* (New York: Viking Press, 1932).

Sartre, Jean-Paul. *La Nausée* (Paris: Gallimard, 1938).

Sayers, Dorothy. "Detective Fiction: Origins and Development." See Burack.

Simenon, Georges. *Chez les Flamands* (Paris: Fayard, 1932).

———. *Maigret et le Corps sans Tête* (Paris: Presses de la Cité, 1955).

———. *Les Mémoires de Maigret* (Paris: Presses de la Cité, 1950).

———. *Pietr le Letton* (Paris: Fayard, 1931).

———. *La Tête d'un Homme* (Paris: Fayard, 1931).

Simon, Claude. *La Route des Flandres* (Paris: Minuit, 1959).

Steeman, Stanislas-André. *L'Assassin habite au 21* (Paris: Champs-Elysées, 1939).

_____. *Crimes à vendre* (Bruxelles: Editions Libres, 1946).

Stout, Rex. "Watson Was a Woman." See Haycraft.

Symons, Julian. *Mortal Consequences* (New York: Schocken Books, 1973).

Taylor, Wendell Hertig. See Barzun.

Thomson, H. Douglas. *Masters of Mystery* (London: Collins, 1931).

Tourteau, Jean-Jacques. *D'Arsène Lupin à San Antonio: le roman policier français de 1900 à 1970* (Paris: Mame, 1970).

Van Dine, S. S. *The Bishop Murder Case* (New York: Scribner, 1929).

_____. *The Greene Murder Case* (New York: Scribner, 1928).

Véry, Pierre. *Les Quatre Vipères* (Paris: Rue François I, 1934).

Vian, Boris. *L'Ecume des Jours* (Paris: Pauvert, 1963).

Wheatley, Dennis. *Murder off Miami* (London: Hutchinson, 1936).

Wilson, Edmund. "Who Cares Who Killed Roger Ackroyd?" See Haycraft.

Wrong, E. M. "Crime and Detection." See Haycraft.

Zangwill, Israel. *The Big Bow Mystery* (New York: Henry, 1891).

Zeltner, Gerda. "Robert Pinget et le roman policier." *Marche Romane*, 21 (1971).

Index of Authors

Index of Titles